EDEN AND AFTERWARD

Eden and Afterward

A Mockingbird Guide to Genesis

By William McDavid

Mockingbird Ministries

Charlottesville, VA

MOCKINGBIRD

Mockingbird Ministries

100 West Jefferson Street

Charlottesville, VA 22902

Cover design by Tom Martin. Editing by David Zahl. Published 2014.

ISBN-13: 978-0615997933

ISBN-10: 0615997937

Thanks to Paul Walker, for his insight into the Bible's 'first dysfunctional families;' Paul Zahl, whose suggestions as a reader helped shape this book; David Zahl, for his careful attention as editor; and Emily Stubbs and Ken Wilson, for their meticulous and tireless proofing.

Contents

Introduction

There's an old story of a Jewish rabbi who once attempted to heal a blind man. After rubbing saliva in the man's eyes and laying hands on him, the rabbi asked if the cure had worked. "I can see people," the man ventured, "but they look like trees, walking." Then, as the account of this healing in the book of Mark puts it, "Jesus laid his hands on his eyes again; and he looked intently and his sight was restored, and he saw everything clearly."*

The most obvious way to look at the healing is as a partially botched job, the first time around, like when a character in the *Harry Potter* books tries to transfigure someone into a cat, but only succeeds in giving their human target whiskers and a tail. But the man's fuzzy, only partially restored vision works as a potent metaphor for the way we view the world around us. We see other people through the lenses of expectations and grudges, biases and resentments. Or perhaps our lens is rose-colored, like the immovable love a parent has for a child.

These resentments and biases and blind spots impair our ability to live. The way we see the world deeply affects our ability to love and feel loved, to forgive others and forgive ourselves. Sin and self-justification often blind us to the way things truly are, and in so doing they damage our relationships with others and with God. Reconciliation in those relationships, giving and receiving mercy, and learning to love lie at the core of our desires as humans. These desires are frustrated by our blindness, so we

---

* Mark 9:23-24. Bible quotations are NRSV.

pray, like another blind man, "My teacher, let me see again" (Mk 10:51).

Stories captivate us because the good ones sharpen our vision. They teach us about the world, about other people, and about ourselves. Good stories can be revisited over and over, throughout one's entire life, and there is always more to see, more to take away. A good story's reserve of truth is inexhaustible, because stories describe our ineffable human experience; we see the meanings of our lives and the things that happen to us blurrily—they appear like trees, walking. So as a story's various images and characters and meanings come into focus ever more sharply, they simultaneously reveal how much meaning continues to elude us.

The stories contained in the book of Genesis are, at worst, brilliant bits of cultural mythology that endure, like the Greek myths, because they express an unspeakable something which lies near the essence of human experience. On the lowest estimation, Genesis has earned its place alongside such literary masterpieces as *The Iliad, The Odyssey,* or *Othello.* Like those works, Genesis has exercised an enduring power to shape one of the world's oldest and most rich cultures, Judaism, to say nothing of its ongoing influence today. But on the highest estimation, Genesis presents something even greater: an exploration of the relationship between God and human beings, a work which cannot lead us astray because it is an authoritative revelation by God himself.

At its lowest common denominator, which is world-class literature, Genesis can be examined for how it works as a story, for its deep reservoir of truth about humanity and, just possibly, God. It can be appreciated by anyone as great literature, and yet it always resists being read as *just* great literature. To the three world religions which hold it in highest esteem, whenever we examine the literary merits of Genesis—just as we would with Faulkner or Hemingway—the book subtly prods us toward reading it as something *more* than just good literature. So although this companion to Genesis will focus upon the stories' symbols, motifs, emotions and characters, the human experience distilled into these narratives will constantly raise new questions, questions of providence and blessing and judgment.

At the heart of these questions lies God's relationship with Israel and, by extension, the way he relates to us today. But we must start with human experience, just as Christianity started with a series of concrete, grounded events, which doctrine then described. So the stories here must come before our ideas about them, must be allowed to shape those ideas rather than vice-versa. They ask us to imagine their sights, sounds and scents, placing us in their characters' shoes and asking us to feel their emotions. When the Bible chooses to speak about God through story, imagination and empathy come first, and analysis comes second.

Both imagination and analysis present certain roadblocks. That is, we cannot fully empathize with the characters; we cannot fully enter into the times and places and situations in which these stories are set. With a book like Genesis, the stories of which are veiled by religious disputes, encrusted with over-familiarity, and often taken for granted, sometimes the story first asks us to register its strangeness, its otherness. No commentary has yet explained everything that happens in Genesis, just as no individual reader of the Bible or other great literature will fail to uncover new meanings with every re-reading. Often, the strangeness of the Bible does not ask us to sharpen our vision of the people who look like trees, but rather to admit they are blurry, to recognize our vision is still foggy and stilted.

Any literary criticism, especially of sacred Scripture, must be flawed for two reasons. First, and most fundamentally, plain words can never explain away a story or substitute for it. At most, they can provide a poor approximation of the irreducible truths of experience, and for this reason, literary analysis at its best does not explain a story so much as provide an entry into it. Ideally, reflection and analysis lead someone to go back to the story and see its images more vividly, to feel its strangeness and mystery ever more acutely.

This is especially true with religious stories, because if plain meaning could substitute for experience, religion would be a mere set of propositions, a list of truths God wanted to reveal in bullet-point fashion. Worse, we would have a God of bare, denuded truth alone, one whose operation in history is meaningful only insofar as it teaches an idea. God's operation in history is of course revelatory, but this revelation itself testifies to *God with us*, taking action in the world for our benefit. And analysis should not decode part of a story and leave a mysterious remainder, as if better criticism might leave less to be explained. Instead, if the analysis is good, it heightens the mystery at every turn.

A second problem is bias, in this case a viewpoint drawing upon Christian theology. Any viewpoint, even at the most basic level, is limited. If I want to see a shoebox, it is impossible to look at it as a whole. I can see three sides at a time at most, and the others are hidden from me. Literary interpretation is no different; we can only see one angle at any given time, and we must do our best to infer the whole from the *particular* part we focus on. This may sometimes be limiting, but it can also be freeing: since we cannot ever know except "in part," as a first-century reader of Genesis once said (1 Cor 13:12), we can look forward to an inexhaustible reservoir of angles and vantage points and meanings, and this "part" can only acquire more depth the more we read. The Bible's figures will always appear blurry, like trees, but the focus may sharpen over time.

This companion to the stories of Genesis focuses on God's gradual, messy, and often convoluted redemption of fallen humanity in history, and this focus imposes a few limits. Creation is omitted because, while it sets the stage for the drama, the relatably human saga begins with the serpent, who provides a sort of "big bang" to the story which kicks off the drama of redemption and the emergence of the human world *as we now know it.* I cannot relate to Adam or Eve before the temptation, but at the moment of the Fall, we see ourselves in them. There are some stories which could easily be included, but are not: for example, the rape of Jacob's daughter, Dina. Much of what's left out is chronology, which works to give the story a grounded, historical feel, to give the nation of Israel a sacred genealogy, and to break up the stories, giving them distance when distance is needed, and immediacy—implying a closer link with the preceding story—when immediacy is needed.

In any companion which is not a line-by-line commentary, some selection is necessary, and this is just one of many lenses which may allow the trees to look slightly more like people, once we turn away from the analysis and back to the story's primal vision. This turning-back is hopefully the end result of any analysis, so references to the stories themselves are included.

Our entry into the story—the long, old story of fallen human beings and God's presence with them—starts with the figure of Adam, who has one foot planted in an idyllic past and another raised up, hesitant, but inexorably stepping down into the confused drama of history. With that strange, mysterious transition from God's ideal world and into ours, the story of redemptive history begins. We pray with Mark's blind man, "My teacher, let me see again."

---

* The idea of the Fall as beginning to 'actualize' human history is drawn from Søren Kierkegaard, *The Concept of Anxiety*, trans Albert B. Anderson and Reidar Thomte (Princeton, NJ: Princeton UP, 1980).

The Fall

(Genesis 3:1-24)

The Fall stands at the beginning of Genesis, and because it is so well known, it is perhaps especially difficult to see with fresh eyes. For instance, sometimes we approach the story from a purely intellectual standpoint, and we're immediately put in a bind: *how* did Adam come to sin? Did God create him with some character trait that would lead him to sin? Or was it more a matter of the serpent's influence ("the devil made me do it!")?* The first conjecture would seem to make Adam's sin God's fault; in the second, it is the serpent's. Either way, Adam's free decision to sin, as well as the guilt which follows it, doesn't come into view.

Luckily though, the Fall is written as a story, so we are given an entirely different way to approach it, one that doesn't run into the same difficulty. We reach the impasse above if we approach it from the top down, but things can start to make (more) sense if we go instead from the bottom up. Which is not to suggest that it will ever, in any perfectly satisfying way, make the kind of sense that can be put into words.

But we'll have to try. A clue to the "why" of the Fall is the serpent's words, "did God really say?" It's not so much an attempt to throw doubt on God as it is an entry into the conversation. Eve knows that God really did say what he said, and when she answers that he did say it, the serpent doesn't argue with her, but presses on to a new point: "You will not die... you will be like God" (3:4-5).

---

* Uncited quotation marks are generally paraphrases or idioms.

Why ask in the first place if God really said it? Eve's memory is perfectly reliable; she's not weak on *that* particular point. But it does open up space for his subsequent appeal to her. I could approach an attractive married woman at a bar and say, "are you *really* married?" My point wouldn't be to make her doubt that she is married; my point would be to suggest that maybe she *shouldn't* be married. It's not doubt about whether or not she is married that I am communicating to her; instead it is a basic sense of incredulity, of injustice that that should be the state of things. So the serpent's query is not so much a disputing whether or not God said what he said as it is a suggestion of a new thought to Eve, a new perspective: it is now possible for her to think that God's prohibition is not a good or natural one, because the serpent doesn't seem to believe it is.

Imagine a married woman, totally happy with her life, content, who has never imagined infidelity because she cannot conceive of life outside her marriage. But then someone asks, "are you *really* married?" Suddenly a new set of possibilities—with their attendant temptations—might open up to her.

That is the best comparison I can think of for Eve and the serpent: the Fall being impossible without him, yet still fully a matter of Eve's sin (and Adam's). The serpent proposes a new possibility to Eve, who accepts it; Eve communicates this new possibility to Adam, who also accepts it. The two are equal in their guilt.

∞∞∞∞∞∞

But what is this new possibility? We look again at the serpent's words: "You will not die; for God knows that when you eat of it your eyes will be opened, and you will be like God, knowing good and evil." This is not an intellectual argument but an emotional one. There's no point-counterpoint, no back-and-forth. It takes just one sentence, because again, he is not giving her an argument or justification. He is suggesting a new set of possibilities for her, and she will carry them into action herself. These possibilities are as follows:

a. She will not die: her life is not in God's hands, subject to his rules, but can now be subject to her own. She will decide what it takes for her to live. We can call this self-sufficiency, the idea that she can look out for her own best interests independently of God. Her basic dependence on God for life is put into question, and now she can take responsibility for herself.

b. She will be like God because her eyes will be opened: not only will she no longer be dependent on God, but also she will be on his level somehow. This appeal is to pride: Eve can become something more than she is. Of course, the desire to be like God denies her place in the world as human. To quote Paul Walker, Rector at Christ Episcopal Church, Charlottesville:

> *"What we call 'the Fall'—the fall from paradise, the fall into a life and world of sin and death—is really a misnomer, I think. The deepest ill represented in our Genesis story is temptation to believe the serpent's words—that we 'will be like God.' Instead of a fall, it is a grasping for something higher, symbolized in Eve's reaching up for the fruit. We see not a fall, but a desire for a kind of spiritual ascendancy."* ("Being Like God Is a Killer," sermon, March 13, 2011)

c. Finally, she will know good from evil. The best sense I can make of this is that Eve did not know she was sinning when she decided to eat the fruit, because she didn't know evil yet. The implication (which we can trace back Augustine, 354-430 CE) is that evil began as a misguided good—the good of the self as independent from God. The knowledge of evil will happen at the exact instant that she acts contrary to God; now that there's a distance between her and God, "evil" is the name given to our tendency to live on our side of that divide. We learn of the difference between good and evil only by acting out evil and learning it firsthand.

Think again of the marriage analogy: the person about to cheat on their spouse doesn't really conceive of it as evil, but as some kind of good—a way to avoid resenting their husband, or a pursuit of what seems like genuine love, or a response to boredom, the need to inject meaning into a stagnant life. It is only at some point during the affair that the knowledge that things are now askew will hit like a ton of bricks. Whatever moral implications of wrongdoing there may be only become totally clear after the fact. This comparison is an inadequate one, and perhaps it points to why Eden is often referred to as a "state of innocence." Our normal, everyday use of the word "innocence" involves having little knowledge (in Eve's case, none) of evil, because we have not yet experienced ourselves committing it. But where our innocence is partial (never cheated, never committed financial fraud, never taken a life, etc.), Adam's and Eve's was total.

These three possibilities are addressed by Eve's desires in the next verse: "So when the woman saw that the tree was good for food, and that it was a delight to the eyes, and that the tree was to be desired to make one wise, she took of its fruit and ate; and she also gave some to her husband, who was with her, and he ate." Good for food, meaning good for self-sufficiency and self-nourishment; pleasing to the eyes, meaning that the objects of our desires will now be the things that build up our pride and make us like God; and good for wisdom—the knowledge of experience, of good and evil. Still, we can only speculate up to a certain point about the reasons for the Fall, because Adam and Eve before the Fall (or in Walker's description, misguided "spiritual ascendancy") were totally different from Adam and Eve after it. We have inherited those differences, so it is impossible to ever really get a handle on the state of innocence.

◇◇◇◇◇◇◇◇

What we can understand, pretty naturally, is the Fall's effects, because they are the air we breathe; they characterize us. And the immediate result is the beginning of physical modesty—the two cover up with fig leaves. The image here is reminiscent of a five-year-old who gets caught misbehaving and immediately covers her eyes with her hands. Our pasts cannot be hidden, but we can hide our physical selves. Covering-up is the natural response to shame, guilt, and knowledge of wrongdoing.

And then there's the idea of separation. Physical modesty always arises out of some distance from the people around us—the primal discomfort of being naked around others happens mainly because it feels too close, encroaching. There is a basic separation between Adam and Eve, Adam and God, and Eve and God that serves as a prerequisite for this modesty.

To keep following the thread, what about the thought of being naked in Times Square on a Tuesday afternoon makes us uncomfortable? The exposure, maybe—but why would exposure make us uncomfortable? It's those feelings that form a natural bridge into the world of the story. Why does anyone ever need to hide?

It's a complicated question with a number of potential answers, but one we could suggest for this story would be uncertainty about whether or not we will be accepted. Again, our bridge into stories is always empathy with the characters, seeing ourselves in them, so we have to think back to that last big screw-up—major—that you have had to cover up, hide. Think for a second. What would your wife (or boss/preacher/kid/brother) say if they knew *that* about you? What would they think?

Feeling our way through this sense of shame and consequent desire to hide it, we see a fundamental tension begin to emerge, one that will be the psychological locus of many of the biblical stories: *there is a tension between the desire to be loved and the desire to be self-sufficient.* If we told our wife/boss/father about that bad decision we made, we fear they might reject us. So we cover up to present our best selves to others. That can inhibit us from being loved, because being loved requires being known. Those of us who like to present to others our illusions of having it all together cringe at the thought of being loved not through strength, but through forgiveness. That is, even if we know things will work themselves out in the end and that someone who sees the worst in us will love us anyway, even then—that doesn't help the fear of coming clean very much. Because the experience of shame will still be there, perhaps even more if we're going to be loved in a new way, a way in which we know at every minute that we do not deserve it.

Of course, this kind of undeserved love can be wonderful, once we get used to it. But at first, we'd so much rather be self-sufficient—that is, have ground of our own to stand on—than be loved in the midst of our shame.

So being truly loved and being self-sufficient are in conflict. Being loved, at its height, means being loved within our weaknesses and failures; being loved in a way that is simultaneous with being known. But being self-sufficient means pretending those weaknesses do not exist; it entails performing and earning.

◇◇◇◇◇◇◇

Modesty comes as the first sign of what will be fallen man's solution to the problem of being loved and being self-sufficient. Hiding, pretentiousness, putting on airs—these are how we now try to earn love. Not surprisingly, they all involve *concealing our weaknesses.* Perhaps I am reading into the story a bit here, but Genesis itself will interpret the symbol of the fig leaves in a similar way, an interpretation carried out in later stories as well.

You have sinned, therefore you must hide that sin. You cover up your professional incompetence or looming bankruptcy or your heavy drinking, your son's depression or the fact that you're in therapy, or the creeping suspicion that your marriage is becoming loveless. Weaknesses like these are not things we like to advertise—usually, they're things we hide from our spouses, parents, children, and sometimes, even from ourselves.

Of course, clothes have a protective function, too—some element of concealment is necessary and can even be good, all things considered. The shame of being fully known is not something that we can bear; even though we are "fully known" (1 Cor 13:12), the art of being vulnerable and defenseless before God is a task for a lifetime. The fact that we're not forced to deal with our shame—indeed, we may not even be aware of our faults—can be a gracious one. Just as Adam fell by denying his limited, creaturely status, some element of human redemption involved re-*dis-cover*ing ourselves as sinners. The theme of clothes as covering who we really are will be reprised throughout the entire Bible, from Joseph's "Technicolor dreamcoat" to Paul's exhortation to "put on the Lord Jesus Christ" (Rom 13:14). The symbol's biblical root is here in Genesis, in the idea of vanity covering over shame.*

The clothing also represents our need to hide our shame from each other, the first "horizontal," or person-to-person, effect of the Fall. Paralleling this is the symbol of "vertical" shame, the need to hide from God. In this, Adam and Eve literally hide behind a tree; again, the best analogy here is probably a child running away after doing something bad, and this biblical passage is the archetype for that sort of shame. The unity between the "horizontal" fig leaves and the "vertical" hiding asserts the strongest connection between the brokenness in our relationship with God and the dysfunction in our relationships with others. People are united in their vulnerability and exposure before God; self-sufficiency is innately individualistic and isolating from others. Here again we see the strangely circular character of the Fall: the need for self-sufficiency drives

---

* The idea that clothes symbolize vanity covering over shame draws from William Wilson, "Adam and Eve", Lecture at The University of Virginia, Fall 2010.

Adam and Eve to eat the fruit, and eating the fruit separates them from each other and from God, thus forcing them to actually be self-sufficient.

◇◇◇◇◇◇◇◇

Another apparent result of the Fall has to do with blame-shifting. Given Adam's and Eve's participation in what has happened, they know that there is guilt; they have become guilty. Try as we might, there is no way to deny the universal reality of guilt; each of us feels it in our shame before the other, and before God. But even though guilt itself cannot be denied, there *is* a way to deny that guilt applies to *me*, and that way is to *localize the reality of guilt in someone else.* More commonly, we call this blame-shifting, and like shame, it can be observed from early childhood on. I tell my parents that the DUI was someone else's fault; I rationalize my son's flunking a course by telling all my friends how Mrs. Johnson always had it out for him; I blame my recent unemployment on my boss's blindness to my ability.

Regardless of whether or not the Fall in Genesis actually happened historically (I personally think it did), its marvelous literary composition testifies to its value. Is anyone exempt from hiding and blame-shifting? And who can deny that hiding our true selves and blaming others for our own shortcomings are at the very root of human dysfunction? The story accomplishes all of these insights—and infinite ineffable others.

Each of us wants to exempt ourselves from the sin of the human race, just like Adam did ("Eve gave me the fruit!") and Eve did ("the devil made me do it!"). By shifting blame, we seek to place ourselves in the "good" camp and others in the "bad." This self-righteous attempt to exonerate ourselves not only fractures friendships and families, but also it's one reason why the church, frequently accused of self-righteousness, has lost credibility in the contemporary world. Some might say this need to form sharp us-them divides plays a major role in nations that have turned violent or totalitarian. One such example of national self-righteousness came with the immensely puritanical Soviet regime, which gradually developed an ideology to make itself the embodiment of all human goodness and progress—which served as a justification for terrible crimes and suffering. A prominent prisoner of that regime, during its most brutal phase under Stalin, rightly saw through the war crimes and horrors to the moral self-justification underneath:

> *"If only it were all so simple! If only there were evil people somewhere insidiously committing evil deeds, and it were necessary only to separate them from the rest of us and destroy them. But the line dividing good and evil cuts through the heart of every human being. And who is willing to destroy a piece of his own heart?"**

In terms of our lives—"practical application"—the story of the Fall is above all else a call to recognize, through our affinity with Adam's self-sufficiency, covering-up, and blame-shifting, our own bias toward denying our dependency and guilt. Recognizing (re-cognizing) our Adamic denial of our own sinfulness, shame and guilt is the empathetic touchstone of the story, as well as a vital step toward a genuinely religious life. We will always struggle to deny it—such struggle is so deeply-rooted that it cannot ever be fully extirpated—yet such a denial only proves, by the logic of Genesis 3, that we are in fact sinners, as it proved that Adam and Eve were. The line runs through our own hearts, too, and recognizing our participation in Adam's sin can ultimately open us to grace, especially for those who believe that God comes specifically for "the sick" (Mk 2:17).

◇◇◇◇◇◇◇◇

One last thought: God curses Eve with pain in childbirth and Adam with futility in work. According to the story, these were the original two callings of humanity—to fill the earth and to subdue it. Now neither will be possible without pain and heavy toil. We will not be able to fulfill our function as human beings perfectly, and our trouble with fulfilling both of these Genesis callings will serve as enacted, lived symbols of weakness and futility: on the negative side, pain and toil, but on the positive side, reminders of the truth that we are not self-sufficient.

Our original theological question was, "Who's to blame? God, for making Adam and Eve capable of sin, or the serpent, for forcing them into it?" Now, through the story's literary sense, this question can finally be properly addressed: The Fall is a reality, we are definitively guilty, and questions about who's to blame only prove that we are truly sinful—and truly responsible. A dark conclusion, to be sure, but no darker than we should expect from a story about how evil, pain, estrangement, shame,

---

* Aleksandr Solzhenitsyn, *The Gulag Archipelago, 1918-1956, Volume I* (New York, NY: Basic Books, 1997).

pride, and betrayal entered the world. Which isn't to say that original sin is, at least not first and foremost, a theological truth to which we give assent. No, it is one to be inevitably, tragically lived out—and for that we turn to Cain and Abel.

Cain and Abel

(Genesis 4:1-26)

Here we follow the second generation of humanity, and we continue to see the effects of the Fall radiating outward. The first result of the Fall, in human relationships, was covering up and the second blame-shifting; the third will be murder. Cain's competition with Abel follows so closely upon the Fall, and his crime is so closely linked with earning God's favor, that a vital connection point with the later stories also emerges, namely, the link between violence/discord and human self-justification. The act of building up one's pride and ignoring one's faults is always, to some degree, spiritual at root.

Adam and Eve saw the tie between them and God unravel, break, snap, crimp, or whatever image you want to use. Their children, Cain and Abel, are the first to be born under the new regime of fallen humanity. So they cannot deny that the vertical relationship has been broken; instead they must seek to tie back themselves to God, to re-link themselves to God's original vision for humanity, to repair their link to God himself. Thus we see the beginning of "re-ligion" (root meaning "tying-back"); its beginnings are as violent as any moment in its subsequent history.

In fact, one helpful definition of "religion" might be the full set of our tyings-back to God, in whatever form they take. In pre-modern times, sacrifice was a default way of pleasing the gods, soothing their anger, and infusing the universe with new life (through death). Much as we might like to do some theological razzle-dazzle and find a way to make sense of sacrifice in a Jewish/Christian context, I'm not sure we can. But perhaps we might understand the practice a little better by approaching it as an ancient ritual, that is, by hazarding some guesses as to what its original practitioners might have had in mind:

a. New life: the thing sacrificed would somehow infuse nature with the force of the life it had yielded. The demand for first-fruits, or the best of every harvest or flock, can be understood as "seeding" nature back with the best, thus giving the next harvest or future animal births an ideal starting-point.

b. Feudal payment: to say "feudal" here may be anachronistic, but this aspect of sacrifice is not unlike acknowledging a landowner, superior, family head, occupying kingdom, etc., by giving a portion of your crops/flock away. In this case, it is God who has given them the land, and they work it under his allowance. They work under Nature's dominion; all they have is borrowed from Nature and its God, and they pay homage to this—or pay their respects—with sacrifice.

c. Closely connected with this would be death: the death of our possessions comes to symbolize and enact our powerlessness before God, our lack of self-sufficiency. In the Jewish religion, this focus on death will become elaborated and deepened in Abraham's covenant ritual with God, the Jewish Passover, and the Law of Leviticus.

◇◇◇◇◇◇◇

But back to the story: both brothers sacrifice, yet God is pleased with one and displeased with the other. This almost arbitrary pleasure/displeasure is the crux of the narrative, especially since God does not, at first, have any reason for preferring one over the other.

Again, in the Genesis account, Cain and Abel are the first two people born after the Fall. They are the first characters in the story who have not experienced anything but the sin and self-justification of life outside of original fellowship with God. Thus they are everyman; their actions and reactions will demonstrate the effects of the Fall, as well as the reality of life after the Fall, in their most stark forms.

In terms of plot, the Fall and expulsion from Eden provide the catalyst for the two brothers' need to sacrifice and "tie-back." God's preference of Abel over Cain will likewise drive the remainder of the story. Neither Abel nor Cain are described much apart from one being a farmer and the other a shepherd, so again, we can safely assume that their actions represent those of the *typical human being after the Fall.* Cain cannot help his murderous rage, and we'll need to look a little more at their internal motivations to understand why.

After God makes his preference of Abel's sacrifice known, Abel becomes a walking judgment on Cain, a living reproach to him. The dynamic we see played out between them is indicative of how *inwardly-directed* human beings become after the Fall. Abiding in a static sort of peace with one another and with God in Eden, they were not conscious of self. Think of a kid playing tennis for the first time, hitting the ball around with a friend, and enjoying a (mostly) uncompetitive time learning something together. The child grows up, continues getting better and better, and soon has some promising offers from Division I collegiate programs. At some point, however, the possibility of failure sets in—or the pressure to maintain success—and the relationship with tennis assumes a darker, more obsessive character. Now, each match reflects a possible value-judgment upon the person who's playing, because her identity has become so wrapped up in the possibilities of success or failure.

After the Fall, as we saw, a sense of shame and failure sets in, and with that shame comes a new consciousness of the self in relation to God. There is no longer a simple and unconscious "love of the game"; the game itself becomes a spectrum of good performance versus bad performance, success versus failure, obedience versus disobedience, righteousness versus unrighteousness. Just like professional sports (or education or a career in finance, etc.), the existence of a spectrum between total religious success, on the one hand, and total failure, on the other, implies that we as humans should work ourselves toward Total Success. In Judeo-Christian terms, this is called the "Law," and an analogy exists in nearly every arena of performance in human life. With the need to self-justify by clawing one's way toward Total Success (or Righteousness), the spectrum quickly becomes a ladder, the ladder meant to tie us back.

Self-consciousness, in the negative sense, is simply a preoccupation with your place on the ladder combined with the desire, and thus pressure, to ascend it. Psychologically, if Abel is the only other man on Earth (as the story is told here), then it would seem as if Cain can be rid of his unrighteousness simply by killing him. That is, if Andre Agassi and I are the only two tennis players alive, and tennis is the crux of both our identities, then he is a constant reminder of my failure at the game, my distance from the ideal. But if I break his leg... well, there's a part of me that would find that tempting.

⬦⬦⬦⬦⬦⬦⬦

God is more pleased with Abel than Cain, and it is difficult to discern why. In the idea of paying homage to God through sacrifice, there is a spectrum. On one end, there is self-renunciation, the death of pride. On the other end, there is sacrifice as a pro-active means to control the world around you, a form of leverage over the divine will. The tension between sacrifice as a grateful gift to God and sacrifice as a means of controlling God's favor abides throughout the Hebrew Scriptures. It is the tension between control and humility.

The human heart has an inherited desire to control God's favor and secure its own righteousness, that is, spiritual value. In the biblical history, self-justifying human hearts are always erring on the side of using sacrifice as a means to control God. Although God commands sacrifices from Genesis on, He continually criticizes sacrifice as a means of control. These criticisms exist in the following passages, among others:

> *"The sacrifice of the wicked is an abomination to the LORD, but the prayer of the upright is his delight." (Prov 15:8)*

> *"The sacrifice of the wicked is abomination; how much more when brought with evil intent." (Prov 21:27)*

So it would appear that sacrifices in themselves are not as important as the character and mentality of the person who brings them; God cannot be bought off. After King David, the "man after God's own heart," slept with a married woman (Bathsheba) and engineered her husband's death, the guilty king wrote a heartfelt critique of sacrifice:

> *"For you have no delight in sacrifice; if I were to give a burnt offering, you would not be pleased. The sacrifice acceptable to God is a broken spirit; a broken and contrite heart, O God, you will not despise." (Ps 51:16-17)*

For David, his wrongdoing is so great that he cannot just throw sacrifices at it. Imagine you were Bathsheba's child by her first husband, and David offered you $10,000 for what he'd done to your family. More insulting than consoling, right? Because he would be trying to gloss over the horrible thing he did and somehow make it right. And it cannot be made right; a heartfelt and tearful apology still probably wouldn't help your feelings toward him much—but it would certainly be a better start than trying to pay you off.

Of course, we don't want to draw too many analogies between the way we work and the way God works, but it does help to explain how some people use sacrifice as a means of controlling God, and why God continually reminds Israel that their sacrifices cannot control him. The one thing we can do nothing to engineer—a broken and contrite heart—is the only thing that can direct us toward God. But it must happen *to* us. David did not realize his wrongdoing until one of his friends and advisers, by telling him a story and brutally forcing him to identify with its villain, finally brought him to a place of genuine brokenness and regret.

∞∞∞∞∞∞

Before we turn back to the Cain and Abel story to see how later Jewish ruminations on sacrifice may shed some light, it is too tempting not to bring a quick element of Christianity into this. The strand of Hebrew religious thought we have been surveying—the critique of sacrifices as instruments of controlling God—was occasionally taken to extremes. One of these extremes came with the brilliant—though arguably deranged—prophet Ezekiel. His critique of human control went so far as to suggest that given man's tendency toward self-justification and mis-use of religion as a means of controlling God's favor toward us, our ultimate hope would lie in *God* making sacrifice to *us*—a very backwards idea:

> "And, thou son of man, thus saith the Lord GOD: Speak unto every feathered fowl, and to every beast of the field, 'Assemble yourselves, and come; gather yourselves on every side to my sacrifice that I do sacrifice for you, even a great sacrifice upon the mountains of Israel, that ye may eat flesh, and drink blood.'" (Eze 39:17)

Christians, as you might imagine, have had a lot to say about this one.

Unfortunately, we've already lost sight of the story itself. Theology is not what the story of Cain and Abel is primarily about. And yet the passages above do shed some light on the tendency to use sacrifice as a way of dictating our standing before God. With that in mind, the trees in this story come a bit more into focus: God's reason for preferring Abel's sacrifice *can* be seen, but only in retrospect.* That is, once Cain kills his brother, he reveals himself to be a ladder-climber. The fact that he was so upset by God's preference of Abel's sacrifice over his own suggests that he was thinking of the sacrifice in terms of tying himself back to God, clawing his way up the religious ladder. Such sacrifices, as the passages above imply, have little value—in fact, they may backfire, as they do here.

◇◇◇◇◇◇◇

Often I'm tempted, as a reader, to identify myself with Abel and grieve over his mistreatment, his near-martyrdom. Unfortunately, the story does not really allow us to do so. We have no idea what was going on in Abel's mind, and he is dead. Moreover, our desire to think of ourselves as people like Abel—the righteous victim—is the same desire of Adam when he claimed to be a victim at the hands of Eve. The need to distance ourselves from Cain in fact proves us to be exactly like he was. Thus the ethical component of the story is not "thou shall not kill," nor is it some form of "try to think of sacrifice and good works as honoring God rather than earning his favor." That would be avoidance of our identity as sinners and would only prove that, like Adam and Cain, we *are* sinners. The only "application" of this passage would be, "see yourself in Cain, recognize his self-justifying image in you."

◇◇◇◇◇◇◇

Before we close, there are a couple of more strands to wrap up. First, Cain receives the same curse as Adam as a result of this murder. The strong parallel between Adam's curse and Cain's implies that it is impossible for us to avoid the sin of Adam, and like Adam, we incur guilt primarily by pursuing our own righteousness. This is a way of describing "Original Sin," or inherited sin, through narrative.

---

* The "retrospective" solution to the question of why God prefers Abel's sacrifice to Cain's draws from William Wilson, "Cain and Abel", Lecture at The University of Virginia, Fall 2010.

Second, Cain is terrified that people will kill him for what he has done. Here we see a new inflection of human self-justifying: killing someone out of a concern for justice. We want to be judges of the sins of others. God protects Cain by marking him with what's basically a "do not kill—divinely protected" sign, which seems a very strange move for God to make on behalf someone who has twice displeased him. The easiest surface-level explanation here would be that God's love and favor are never completely gone, and even Cain is part of his chosen people. That seems true and works theologically, but God's counterintuitive protection of Cain provides another, final clue to the movements of the story, and perhaps another signpost toward its meaning.

If anyone kills Cain, God promises him, "vengeance shall be taken on him sevenfold" (4:14). Why would people want to kill Cain as punishment for his murder of Abel? Given the sketch of human instincts and psychology, post-Fall, that we have seen so far, one answer above all suggests itself. Cain is a reminder of our self-justifying instincts, our ability as humans to commit murder out of a need to think well of ourselves. On the surface, anyone who murders Cain is placing himself above Cain, denying the equal amount of sin in himself. Again, our perception of each other is colored by our own self-justification projects, and so we are tempted to label Cain as an uncommon sinner. A sinner he is, but not an uncommon one.

Human justice often functions on the assumption that the human race can remain functional and moral as long as we sequester, punish, or kill the "bad people" out there. This assumes that they are the problem, and we are not. Such dualisms are tempting to buy into, because believing in categories of conservatives and liberals, saints and sinners, white and black, Jew and Gentile, educated and uneducated, allows us to be on the "correct" side of such divides. While justice, in terms of punishment, imprisonment, etc., is necessary in many cases, that necessity does not somehow cancel the self-justifying component of human justice. It is irrepressible.

The irony of human justice, in Cain's case, is that killing him would be an act of self-righteousness and moral pretension—an attempt to assure ourselves that we occupy a higher place on the righteousness spectrum. Thus anyone who kills Cain would be guilty of the exact same sin, and for many of the same reasons. Human justice, in a fallen world, cannot help but repeat sin in the attempt to get beyond it. As we've seen, the attempt to get beyond sin, or the thought that we can rise above it, *is* sin itself.

◇◇◇◇◇◇◇◇

In some way, the opposite of murder is empathy. Murder—and along with it, blame-shifting, self-justification, etc.—arises from the need to distance ourselves from our identity as sinners. The opposite is admitting this identity, "hugging the cactus," in the language of Alcoholics Anonymous. While the stories in Genesis aim to communicate varying emotional truths, they almost always invite us to identify with the figure of the sinner. Distancing ourselves from sinfulness only repeats the sins of Adam and Cain. Or as Jesus later put it, "with the judgment you make you will be judged" (Mt 7:2). As dark as this may sound at first, the strand of Judaism he founded ultimately taught that identifying with sin is the one way humanity might overcome it (2 Cor 5:21).

Noah and the Flood

(Genesis 6:1–9:29)

In 1994, when I was too young to remember much, our house flooded after weeks of heavy rain. My parents didn't have time to get much out of the house, so decades-in-the-making record collections, favorite pieces of furniture, and memorabilia years in storage were destroyed. The water kept rising and rising, finally invading the house and flooding all the way up to the second floor, and there was nothing to be done. We were utterly helpless. Most disconcertingly, a friend of my mother's was an acclaimed maker of extremely lifelike dolls. We had been storing them by the hundred for her; when we returned to our house after a couple of months, the dirty, distorted doll figures were scattered at random around the yard.

As readers of Faulkner's story "Old Man" or, more tragically, survivors of tsunamis or hurricanes like Katrina (2005) will know, water is a primal and uncontrollable agent of chaos. It rises and falls almost arbitrarily, destroying some things while leaving others mostly intact, scattering fragments of possessions from an old life at random. In a time when we are technologically advanced enough to have levies, dykes, drainage systems, and cruise-liners, to engage a story like Noah's Ark we may need to stretch our minds to imagine the primal destructiveness of water. Or perhaps one needs only to look at pictures from Hurricane Katrina, or note the deeply ingrained terror elicited by waterboarding, to see water again as an agent capable of unspeakable destruction, one over which humans ultimately have little control.

We can remember too the creation story in Genesis 1, in which God brought the world into being by separating the earth's waters into the firmament above and the sea below; we can remember the symbolism of death in Christianity's sacrament of baptism, or we can look at the book of Revelation's coming of the antichrist figure from out of the sea or, correspondingly, remember God's promise to Revelation's visionary: "the sea shall be no more."

The ocean specifically, and to an extent water in general, are genetically-inscribed symbols of death and chaos, and the biblical authors—like many others—are conscious of water's threat. Grasping the primal terror of water is essential to reading the Noah story.

Seeing water this way allows us to view the flood not merely as a plague or judgment—though it functions as both—but to go beyond that and see water as a literal *reversion to the chaos which existed before creation.* In other words, the safe space that God the Creator carved out in between the waters has been removed; we have no refuge. The dolls from my flooded home are suggestive of the horror: Noah may have been spared, but his home was destroyed, and corpses and other random, senseless detritus are scattered about as he looks outward from the ark.

◇◇◇◇◇◇◇

We could identify this story with a strand which runs throughout Genesis—and later the entire Bible—concerning judgment. Earlier religions would often equate drought, crop plagues, or other natural disasters with religious failings. Nature seemed arbitrary, and religion was arguably first developed, at least in part, as an attempt to manage the violence and unpredictability of nature. When a drought would happen, for some reason it made more sense to claim that it was *us* who failed rather than recognizing our powerlessness in the face of nature.

The idea that the morality of our actions can directly influence nature is a notion that we now know to be false. Many modern thinkers have dismissed religion altogether because the idea of meteorological control was one of religion's early foundational assumptions. In this story, God floods the world to cleanse it from unrighteousness. What makes this Jewish inflection on natural disaster different from broader religious superstition?

Implicit in this story is the idea that *human sinfulness unravels the fabric of creation.* Remembering the flood's meaning as a reversion to chaos, we could say that sin creates so much chaos in the world, makes it deviate so much from God's Edenic vision, that undoing creation and starting over makes more sense than trying to improve the situation. Indeed, the situation cannot be improved. Try as they might, people do not seem to get better or become more righteous. Other ancient religions promised stop-gap solutions—sacrifice more goats next year and maybe the harvest will be better—but the flood implies that nothing less than a total obliteration of the status quo will make things better. Purification comes about through a total death, and then a restoration. God accomplishes both.*

So what we see here is a death of a world, brought about by human sinfulness. God's judgment here isn't so much punishment as a desire to remake things, rehabilitate them. And things are so bad that rather than be improved, they must be destroyed and remade.

∞∞∞∞∞∞

The effects of sin are chaos and disorder. But there's another component here. In the time leading up to the flood, Genesis pretty clearly implies that there were part-human, part-divine beings walking around—mighty men, or "Nephilim," with divine blood. (This can be taken as literal history, but it certainly doesn't *have* to be taken that way.) Thus one way to interpret the Flood is as a judgment on humanity's pretensions to be gods, with the part-divine Nephilim destroyed, while the all-too-human Noah is spared.

Going back to the image of the untamable sea, the flood enacts a complete loss of control upon the world. That is, the human urge to pacify the world around us is revealed to be ridiculous. God is not seen as someone subject to our management; he is portrayed as someone who destroys our illusion of control utterly. We are not gods, and we cannot reckon with gods. We rely solely upon grace. God, in other words, is the Actor—we are passive.

God judges the world for wickedness, specifically for "violence"—the use of force to dominate other human beings. We see the self-justifi-

---

* Christianity, much later, would integrate this idea in its focus on death and resurrection, typified in Christ's death and resurrection and the believer's baptism.

cation which started with Cain now wreaking havoc upon the world. Remembering that the cause of Cain's murder was a desire to please God, the forces of judgment and grace will deal with violence by reminding us that first, God is above all—only he has any power in the face of nature's rapid changes. Second, grace will elevate Noah, but only after he has experienced his passivity as a creature, his dependence upon God's favor.

∞∞∞∞∞∞∞

Fast forward to the "day after," though, and nothing has really changed—Noah passes out after a big night, naked, and one of his sons publicly embarrasses him about it. So what did the flood really accomplish, if things just went back to the way they were?

What we see with the flood is a failed new beginning, at least in terms of human behavior. We will see this theme over and over again in the Bible: God brings a new, holy (meaning "set apart") nation out of Egypt, and they transgress so badly that no one alive during the Exodus will be allowed to see the Promised Land. Israel undergoes cycles of divine deliverance, followed by periods of law-keeping and obedience, followed by disobedience and idolatry, followed by another period of judgment and desolation. Divine deliverance, it would seem, does not imply a change in human behavior.

Noah is spared not so much to remake humanity, then, but because he "alone is righteous before me in this generation," as the Lord says in the story (7:1). It is unclear what makes Noah righteous, and it is fitting that the story doesn't provide more detail—the focus is on God's action, not human action.

∞∞∞∞∞∞∞

With evil and chaos and destruction symbolically identified with water, we see Noah's ark as a symbol here of God's providence. Completely at the mercy of the elements, and yet protected. Powerless in the sense that Noah has no control, but a powerlessness giving him no other option than reliance upon grace. Just as separating the waters in creation made a safe haven for humanity, when this safety collapses, God's gracious favor is there, like a raft, providing a safe and inhabitable space amidst the chaos.

Of course, we can't forget the primal horror of the flood—floating carcasses of animals, seasickness, probably horrendous hygiene and cramped quarters and, I would imagine, a devastating loneliness as every inch of Noah's familiar world is submerged. Even under the protection and favor of God, things can be terrible. And there is no assurance whatsoever that things will get better—except for a promise, a word which may be gracious in content, but a word which we are incapable of ever being fully consoled by.

Again, the Hebrews' later exile to Babylon, slavery in Egypt, and wandering in the desert are all foreshadowed here. The pillar of smoke and fire which accompanies the Israelites in their wandering will be the symbol of God's promise and presence and favor, yet it is a symbol amidst extremely trying circumstances. In the forty years wandering in the desert, a promise of the Promised Land is all the assurance the Israelites have, and it's a promise far distant, one which therefore seems irrational.

God's promise to spare Noah, as the entire world is destroyed by water, is confirmed when a dove brings back an olive leaf. And when Noah returns to land a bit later, God "commits" to creation as it is. In this committal, we see another instance of God choosing the imperfect, giving a promise he cannot break in exchange for a human promise which man cannot keep. The forces of judgment and grace will no longer be enacted through nature, but instead God will deal with his chosen people in the more personal form of a covenant.

A covenant is a solemn promise between two people or groups, usually exchanging obligations. In this covenant, God promises not to destroy every living thing ever again, and he promises that nature will operate predictably: day and night, fall and spring, summer and winter. Nature's stability is guaranteed by God, and this stability is a gift, something that can be relied upon. God gave Adam an obligation, and Adam broke it; now, God takes an obligation upon himself.

This covenant, as with all covenants between the Bible's God and humans, is asymmetrical. Normally, in covenants or contracts, if I break my end of the deal, then you are released from your obligation to me. But here God gives the promise first, and he only lays out our duties afterward. *The promise is not dependent on how well we hold up our end of the bargain.* God's faithfulness always exceeds and outweighs our unreliability.

God will never again destroy every living creature, "for the inclination of the human heart is evil from birth" (8:21). In other words, judgment alone cannot remake the world.

◇◇◇◇◇◇◇◇

God also re-establishes Noah as a new Adam—"Be fruitful and multiply, and fill the earth" (9:1). Like the old one, this new Adam will fail, but the faithfulness of God remains unchanging. God has committed himself, irrevocably, knowing that Noah will be fickle. Human life remains the same as it was before the great flood, but now it will be lived within the context of a promise from God. As the Bible moves forward from this point on, we'll see the promises of God increasing. For now, he will not destroy every living thing ever again. But later, he'll add to that a Promised Land, a promise to be with a chosen people, and a promise to make Israel a great nation.* While humans continue their cycles of rebellion and disobedience, God continues committing himself more and more. Again, there is an excess of God's faithfulness over our response to it.

We have here too the beginnings of what might be called Jewish religion. That is, while other gods were identified largely with nature's changes, the God of Noah will deal with his people more personally, and he will deal with them through a specific set of rites and commandments. The first of those commandments is given here: blood cannot be eaten. Instead of cosmic punishment, blood (where the life resides—9:4) will be drawn out of the meat first. God says he will require it from animals, and here we have perhaps the first suggestion in the Hebrew Scriptures of blood as a payment to God, a sacrifice. Other biblical books talk much more explicitly about the religious significance of blood, but here it is worth noting that it's possibly something of a substitute for dramatic divine judgment. The requirement for blood and the promise to not destroy the world are co-incident; they come together.

Also, God puts a rainbow in the sky. The bow would've been identified with a bow and arrow, one of the main weapons of the time. Christians have sometimes interpreted the bow pointing upward as a sign that God would punish himself rather than humans; his weapon was pointed away from earth. There's nothing that seems wrong or bad about this in-

---

* Whether this last promise is to be interpreted geopolitically or figuratively and spiritually has been the subject of some debate for both Christianity and Judaism.

terpretation, but probably a more direct way to view it would simply be that God has dropped his weapon: put it away, up in the sky and pointed away from us. That is, God gave Noah not only a promise not to destroy the world with water, but also a sign, a visible reminder that he will spare us the worst of his judgment.

◇◇◇◇◇◇◇◇

There is a final point to be made about the strange episode in which one of Noah's children walks in on him naked. This immediately recalls the story of Adam and Eve, when they were embarrassed by each other's nakedness (as a result of the Fall) and felt the need to cover up.

Noah's son Ham finds his father uncovered and calls in his brothers to see. We can probably get a window into this predicament by imagining the same situation in our time. Dad's drunk and naked—do you look away and cover him up, or do you call in your siblings to let them see how funny and embarrassing this is?

The idea that being exposed is indecent can be a hard sell to us 21st-century people. Nude beachgoers, for instance, seem kind of free and unselfconscious in a good way. Still, few of us would want our sons to walk in on us drunk and naked, so Ham's action here probably does cross some lines.

On the surface, the easiest way to read this passage is skipping ahead a little and seeing that Ham was the father of the Canaanites, one of the main peoples from whom the Jews took possession of Israel. Noah's curse of Ham thus works as something of a rationale, or justification, for the later Hebrew war on them; it explains the Canaanites' dispossession of the land.

But returning to Adam and Eve, nakedness symbolizes shame—the shame of being exposed as a fragile, mortal, fallible, fleshly human being.* The fig leaves are identified with human vanity, or the need to pretend we are not mortal and human. Our vanity is sinful, because it is pretentious, but God gave skins to Adam and Eve anyway, because they needed them. All that to say, it seems somehow important for people to have their vanity. Regardless of whether or not Noah deserved his dignity here, he gets it. At the risk of too easy an identification, perhaps this is

---

* Julia Kristeva's essay "Powers of Horror," which discusses our aversion to reminders of our mortality, is an interesting window into our discomfort with reminders of our fragility.

not that different from letting someone with an inflated opinion of herself keep it. Going around and pointing out that people are weak, sinful mortals is not a great social or evangelical posture. God will accommodate himself, at times, to human pride—he works slowly, after all—and we accommodate ourselves to others' pride. Maybe that isn't always such a bad thing, but we are getting into unduly speculative territory.

⬦⬦⬦⬦⬦⬦⬦

Going back to our imaginative "walking in on Dad" scenario, it's easy to imagine Ham's action here as a little righteous, placing his father below him as an object of derision. He fails to acknowledge his dependence for life upon his father, which adds up to an assertion of independence from the person who made him. Furthermore, given the dependence Noah was forced to experience, it's not a stretch to view derision of one's father as a disavowal of God—the role of fathers will parallel divine creativity, authority, favor and judgment for many of the children in Genesis.

We could even say that this episode is an early example of making a connection between respect of father and respect of God, something that will be formalized, much later, in Israel's Ten Commandments. Instead of taking the opportunity to lord over their father, the other two brothers look away, perhaps embarrassed along with him. They came from their father and have no existence apart from him; in turning away, they renounce their moral superiority and instead identify with him—thus acting out the paradigm of dependence which has emerged as the proper relation of man to God.

Noah's children are a "mixed bag"—two respect him and one does not. Noah curses Ham after he wakes up, telling him that he and his children will be slaves. We are told that Ham was the father of Cush, Egypt, Put, and Canaan, each an ancestor of a strong empire.* The power of these civilizations would sometimes bring them into conflict with Israel, and Ham's pride and independence already symbolize the pretensions of human power apart from God, which brought on the flood in the first place. Ham is cursed here for rejecting his relationship of dependence to a father; he separates himself from Noah, and it is only through being humbled that he can learn his weakness and, perhaps, be restored. We are not given any knowledge about the rest of Ham's life here, but the

---

* See Jeremiah 46:7-12

flood itself exemplifies God's power to bring the world to its knees, first in suffering and second in prayer.

◇◇◇◇◇◇◇◇

God places a physical sign in the sky, assuring the world that our dependence upon him is no longer sustained through judgment, but through his permanent promise *not* to destroy us. After judgment, in other words, promise and grace follow.

People will forget, or choose to ignore, the memory of God's judgment as quickly as Ham disregarded Noah. But despite what goes on below it, the bow remains in the sky, affirming irrevocably God's presence and promise.

The Tower of Babel

(Genesis 11:1-9)

"The act of Creation is not an act of power. It is an abdication... it is a kingdom from which God has withdrawn. God, having renounced being its king, can only enter it as beggar."

—Simone Weil, *"Are We Struggling for Justice?"*

So far, Genesis has explored a surprisingly broad range of topics: the origins of sin against God; the advent of the "blame game"; the birth of evil; the beginnings of competition, religion, and violence; divine judgment and promise; the human tendency toward moral relapse; and the religious significance of family life. God destroyed the world in the flood as a result of human wickedness, especially violence, which started with Cain wanting to outdo his brother. But as thinkers like Hobbes and Rousseau noted, the violent war of "all against all" couldn't last forever. At some early point in human existence, collaboration began to make more sense than outright individual competition. People found that they could better defend themselves and prosper in groups, and civilization was the result.

In the story of the Tower of Babel, group pride, not individual pride, will be the problem requiring divine attention. A large group of people find themselves together on a plain, all sharing the same language and possessing the ability to use brick and mortar. They decide to build an enormous tower, reaching up to the heavens, and their motivation for doing so is a desire to make a name for themselves—that is, to become

famous and respected. They want a lasting achievement to commemo-
rate their culture, especially in view of the fact that they may be scattered. They want a legacy.

God intervenes in their plans, confusing their languages and scattering them to different parts of the earth, presumably because "this is only
the beginning of what they will do; nothing that they propose to do will
now be impossible for them" (v 6). The literal reading of this story is a
difficult but unavoidable one: God feels "threatened," in rivalry with
humans, and he must prevent them from becoming too powerful.

Theologically speaking, God's being and power *cannot* be threatened;
he is not like the Egyptian god Osiris, who was supposedly killed and
cut up into pieces. Since God is by definition unchanging, nothing can
threaten him. But the story does not work on a theological, philosophi-
cal, or academic level. It works on a literary one, and for the purposes of
the story, God does seem threatened.

So what exactly threatens him? According to the Adam and Eve narrative, humans are stewards of the earth, acting out their power under God.
In later sacrifices, they pay homage to God, respecting him as the ultimate
source of authority. When we first became violent and rebellious, God was
able to give the world a new start by flooding the earth. But now he has
obligated himself to give us space—he has hung up his bow and promised
that he will not flood the world again.* The Lord's glory, now that destruction has been renounced, lies in his being worshiped by humans.

◇◇◇◇◇◇◇◇

"They will be able to do anything." The story gives us an image not
unlike Atlantis, the image of an awe-inspiring first civilization now lost.
With only a single language, extraordinary cooperation, and technical
expertise, Babel represents a pinnacle of human achievement—a thriving, flourishing, utopian civilization. To have all of humanity at peace
among themselves, living and working together, is a perfect dream, perhaps only equaled in its grandeur by the Leninist vision of Communism
or Dostoevsky's Grand Inquisitor story, which lays out a vision for universal happiness and religious unity.

How would such a civilization threaten the divine? To understand, we

---

* This sounds perhaps crude and overly literal. Parts of it are, again, theologically simplistic or improper, but this is the language and imagery we are given in the stories, and however proper or
improper the language, they express something utterly true.

need to back up a little. In the space between the heavens, carved out by God and guaranteed from flood, humans may assert control. In a certain sense, the thriving of civilization is inevitably connected to human pride and self-sufficiency.

What we have here is the first account of "Babel," identified with Babylon, the greatest of ancient civilizations. Babylon became one of the Israelites' main enemies. And it is the pride of Babylon and its kings which makes the Israelite prophets continually condemn it.[*] Historically, Babylon ended up subjugating Israel and making it a vassal nation, even taking its population captive. The flourishing of human civilization cannot help but give us power, and power always tends toward domination. While Israel, during its high points, understood itself as subsisting only on God's favor, Babylon had a more tangible and, in human terms, more reliable power base: money, military, expertise.

Thus Babylon works as a symbol for a universally human urge toward power: a will to power, as Nietzsche put it, or a lust for domination, in Augustine of Hippo's terms.[†] The Babylonian lust for *political* domination *over other human beings* is thus identified with a universal human desire to *dominate the world and God*. Even when humans are at peace with each other—as seems to be the case here—violence does not disappear. The need to make a name for ourselves is also a desire to make ourselves objects of worship, and thus it crowds out, so to speak, the worship of God.

When human culture can protect and provide for itself, and when "anything becomes possible" for it, God's ability to communicate himself to us as Provider, Protector, and Rescuer is clouded over, compromised. So in Babel we do have a legitimate threat to God's glory on the earth. Other images support this: the language of a tower reaching, metaphorically, to "the heavens" hints at a human assault upon God's majesty, and one meaning of the word "Babel"—a gate to heaven—gets at this, too. Humans are implicitly claiming divine status and, in so doing, are trying to replace God.

◇◇◇◇◇◇◇◇

How does this rather bizarre story match up with the other episodes we've looked at? For starters, once the "horizontal" human-to-human

---

* See Isaiah 13 and Revelation 17.

† "*Libido dominandi*"—a play on words meaning roughly a "lust for mastery which itself masters us."

problems of murder, blame-shifting, and embarrassment are overcome, the "vertical" problems of relating to God only come into sharper focus. Adam's Fall is also confirmed: even in an Edenic civilization, Eden is past. Whatever paradise can be created on human terms, it still cannot bring us back into a true utopia. For its exposure of the dark side of human cultural pretensions, we could possibly even call this story the first piece of dystopian literature.

So Eden is gone, and we cannot return. In Eden, human power (in our capacity as stewards) was synonymous with honoring God and worshipping him. After Eden, human power often comes at the expense of divine glory. Our self-justification detracts from God's manifestation of his glory. For human power to glorify God, it must be understood not as achievement (as was Babel) but as *gift*.

And in reality, human power is never self-sufficient, but always transient and subject to defeat. In the story's terms, God ensures that it can never be understood as self-sufficient. That is, first, it is subject to him—he scatters them—but second, it is subject to other humans. In scattering the nations and giving them different languages, God ensures that humans will be divided and, in being divided, will be subject to competition.

As we know all too well, political power is fundamentally transient— Persia fell to Alexander the Great, the Romans were destroyed by a series of Gothic migrations/invasions, the Holy Roman Empire, the Second French Empire, the Dutch Golden Age... all are gone. Regardless of whether we read this as a historically accurate account of why we have different, competing civilizations, it illustrates a central point about the fickle nature of human power. And it suggests that a perfect civilization would be, religiously speaking, kind of a bad thing; we are incapable of thriving without becoming narcissistic about it. The scattering at the end of the story is a political/cultural version of the curse of Adam, and later writers in the same tradition will return to this theme (e.g. Daniel 2-4, Revelation 17).

It is also worth noting that later in the Jewish tradition, as religious thinkers became disillusioned by Israel's failure to achieve sustained political dominance, some writers suggested that a utopian political culture could only be achieved by God's extreme intervention in human history. Daniel 7-12 exemplifies this conviction, and later Christianity would build on this idea in "Apocalyptic" literature such as the book of Revelation, especially in that work's vision of a new, perfect city coming down to earth in chapter twenty-one. Given how pessimistic Genesis has been about human nature so far, it should not come as a surprise that cultural achievement is seen as something which is always, at least in part, self-justifying, prideful, and dysfunctional. Which isn't to be moralistic; only to be honest.

∞∞∞∞∞

On the one hand, this story's statement that "nothing... will now be impossible" is a sweeping, total affirmation of human potential; on the other, this potential often miscarries in the wrong context. The pessimism here may seem condemnatory from a human point of view, but it only condemns the same pride which led to strife between Adam and Eve, competition between Cain and Abel, and violence. To reject the possibility of utopia on this earth is to open up a space for dependence upon God, a dependence which—as we'll see in the next story—may produce freedom and new beginnings.

Abram: Call, Journey, and Covenant

(Genesis 12:1-15:21)

The Noah story ended with God, who first created humans out of nothingness, promising not to destroy the earth with water, not to return creation to the chaos which preceded it. In this way, the promise was an "election" of all of creation, a covenant with them. God's covenant with Noah was a baseline, almost minimal promise to spare him destruction; as Genesis continues, however, God's covenant with man becomes more specific and more constructive. By the end of Exodus, the "Mosaic" covenant will be a well-defined, well-developed covenant with a nation. His choice, or election, of Abram is one of several stages of God becoming more and more present with a people—and his promises become more developed as this early narrative of Israel progresses.

After human civilization disperses into different cultures following the Tower of Babel, God's presence with his creatures must take the form of presence with *one* person, one people. This person will eventually become a nation, and this nation's prophets, in later books, will occasionally express the ambitious hope that *all* nations will come to worship its God and be included in his promises. But before he becomes an object of any world religion, God will show his distinct character in relation to a single person.

The four stories we have examined thus far form a sort of pre-history—Hebrew legends and mythologies that, of course, may well be true. But Abram is meant to be taken more historically, as a concrete founder of the Jewish nation. And just as Adam's sin spread to the next generation, and in so doing it compromised the entire world (the Flood) and human culture (Babel), God's choice of Abram will spread to the next generation, to a culture (the Jews) and the whole world ("by your offspring shall all the nations of the earth gain blessing" 22:18). Abram will be a new Adam, Adam's inverse; Abram will do through grace and patience and dependence what Adam did through works and impatience and misguided in-dependence.

◇◇◇◇◇◇◇◇

At the end of Babel, humans fractured into different languages and, therefore, cultures and civilizations. The scattering and subsequent wandering of different cultures recalls a political point from the Babel story: God scatters humans to prevent pride and self-reliance with regard to cultural achievement and power. The story of Abram follows almost directly after this one, separated only by a list of descendants. They are placed as closely together as possible while maintaining a sense of historical distance. The upshot of this proximity is that Abram's call to be a nomad mirrors the scattering of nations. The curb against pride which God applied to human culture will now apply to a human person, an individual nomad. Accordingly, the theater of God's action will narrow from political bodies, cultures, and the world into the sphere of the family.*

On the world stage, as we saw in Babel and as Exodus will point out, power is the currency of success. Nations preserve themselves, expand their influence, and keep themselves going with power. For this narrower stage of the family, however, sex lies at the center, the beginning of attraction between parents and the source of children. Sex is required to preserve the family, expand it through wives and children and the relations which grow out of them, and keep families going by providing an heir. Thus we will be more concerned with sex in this and the next seven stories—the "family history" of Israel—than we were in the preceding ones. As power held apart from God blunted his glory in the world by giving cultures the illusion of self-sufficiency, so sex threatens to foster the idea that one can keep a family going without God. We will see as much in Abram's and Sarah's infertility, and later in the requirement for circumcision.

---

* This holds true for all of Genesis, with the exception of Sodom and Gomorrah. Only in Exodus will it start to broaden again into the sphere of political bodies and cultures, as God calls Abraham's descendants—themselves a nomadic people with deep roots in the stories of Abraham, Isaac, and Jacob—out of Egypt.

Here, at the beginning of this "family history," it is worth noting a few things about sex as it is presented in Genesis. The natural starting point is God's mandate to Adam to "fill the earth," in which we see procreation as a natural part of being human. After the Fall, modesty sets in, as Adam and Eve cover themselves with fig leaves. As we noted in that story, the two felt ashamed not merely before God for their sin, but also in front of each other. Modesty implies shame, a reluctance to be physically judged and, at a deeper level, resistance to being known as a human, a mortal, fleshly, fragile, and utterly un-godlike creature. Additionally, our tendency to be modest already implies that something is off about the way humans relate to each other sexually. As later stories will imply, now that humanity is trying to be self-sufficient after Adam, procreation also takes on a self-justifying character. In fact, Genesis almost parallels Darwinism in its suggestion that the human libido cannot be divorced from the instinct to procreate; even in cases where children are practically undesirable and people are using forms of birth control, the sexual instinct still derives, biologically speaking, from a hardwired drive to promulgate the species. Again, the idea of natural selection confirms this beyond a religious context.

Because procreation, after the Fall, is co-opted by self-justification and self-sufficiency, sex too can become selfish. That is, the ingrained drive to have children—which after the Fall is always, at least in part, a selfish one—risks using another's body merely to perpetuate one's own genes. Modesty might be understood, then, as resistance to being used in this way, which is perhaps one reason why feeling loved and accepted is the antidote to modesty; one no longer has to hide their (literal and metaphorical) humanness and vulnerability, and is confident in not being used. In the case of Abram, sexual infertility will symbolize and enact his inability to be self-reliant within the family and, by extension, his reliance upon God for family and progeny. We'll see him forced to accept such reliance upon God in this story, try to do things his own way with Hagar in the next story, and finally accept his dependence upon God in dramatic fashion when God calls him to sacrifice his son.

∞∞∞∞∞∞

This story opens with our hero, who has spent much of his life in Sumeria, a "cradle of civilization." From there, a voice in his head starts telling him to do things. Of course, it could be an apparition, or some miracle he sees, or a priest or shaman—the text doesn't say—but we're forced to consider the strangeness of it, the near-insanity of going out into the wilderness because a god told you to do so. This God claims to be *for* Abram, rewarding people who treat him well and punishing people who treat him poorly. His command, "go," is simultaneously a promise—"I will." The surface-level absurdity of this command/promise immediately reveals two aspects about God: (1), his gratuitousness, the fact that he does not operate within any realm of human predictability, except for (2) that of promise, promise to be *for us*. Abram is called to travel blindly in the wilderness—away from human culture, human transactions, economies of power and influence—but it is in this remote place where God will manifest himself precisely in his characteristics of *gratuity* and *promise*.

Furthermore, God's promise is open-ended. He calls Abram merely to go "to the land that I will show you," without specifying where that land is. Thus the command, which includes the promise, is not something Abram can merely *do* to reap the promised benefits. Rather, God must be there every step of the way, and Abram will never come to a place where he can practice "religion," or carry out commands, independently of God. The voice in his head doesn't tell him, "Go to Antarctica and I'll make you great," but simply, "Go, and I will make you great." As a first-century scholar of the Hebrew Scriptures would later write, "Hope that is seen is not hope" (Rom 8:24); the very vagueness of God's call ensures that Abram will not hope in some predictable destiny, a specific, tangible land of milk and honey, but only in the reliability of the promise and the goodness of the character of the God whom Abram has encountered.

Abram, with his wife and nephew and possessions all in tow, doesn't find out where he is going even after he leaves, but he journeys "by stages" (12:9). We see a fumbling, faltering pilgrimage, again one defined not by some goal, but rather by years of something which must have felt like guesswork, settling down somewhere and then, after weeks or months or longer, growing restless and deciding that, after all, maybe this isn't where God wanted him to settle for good—and packing up once again. Along the way, God shows him Canaan—the "Promised Land"—and promises it to his descendants, but God neglects to give him a good strategy for how to help that promise along. In lieu of more definite plans, Abram is finally compelled by necessity, when a famine comes, to go to Egypt, where—rumor has it—there's extra grain.

∞∞∞∞∞∞

Of course, wandering from place to place is difficult, and despite his admirable persistence, eventually the temptation to be self-reliant comes into the picture. In Egypt, back in a well-developed, civilized world, Abram feels he must fight to preserve his place. The immediate threat is his beautiful wife, a foreigner to the Egyptians, with a foreign husband who cannot defend himself and toward whom Pharaoh's men feel no obligation. Killing him and taking her to be the wife of some powerful Egyptian seems a likely scenario, so Abram, to put it bluntly, effectively prostitutes her to Pharaoh in return for the safety of knowing they won't kill him. And Pharaoh's men, for good measure, add enough slaves and livestock to make him rich into the bargain. Soon Abram, through cleverness and resourcefulness, has found considerable wealth and power (13:2) in one of the richest societies in the world. To say that, at this point in his life, Abram was a person of faith, or that he was placing a high premium on the voice from Ur, would be grossly misguided.

And yet God's promise remains, over and above Abram's response to it. As Karl Barth once said, "The man with whom we have to do in ourselves and in others, though a rebel, a sluggard, a hypocrite, is likewise the creature to whom his Creator is faithful and not unfaithful."[*] That may be a rather fancy theological statement, but this story is one of the first places we see this truth played out. Human disobedience takes place *within* God's promise, and this promise will shape history at a higher level than human obedience or lack thereof. So God, presumably unasked by Abram, on his own initiative, afflicts Pharaoh's family and attendants and staff with plagues—boils, to be specific. Though he is a nomad, Abram's protection is God's providence, and this providence is more powerful than the greatest human civilizations.

There are a couple more things to consider here. First, the plagues are not man-made, but natural. As in the flood story, nature's unpredictability and unmanageability serve as instantiations—or concrete instances of—the limits of human control. The greatest ruler in the world cannot do any more about an unsightly profusion of sudden boils than anyone

---

[*] Karl Barth, *The Humanity of God* (Louisville, KY: Westminster John Knox Press, 1960), 60.

else can. As in the flood, nature symbolizes and instantiates God's power over and above humanity's. Further, God has power over human culture, as we saw in the Babel story, and can rearrange it whenever it conflicts with his promises. This power will come to be a defining factor in Israel's identity: he will once again thwart the most powerful civilization in the world to bring the Jewish nation out of its captivity to Egypt. The parallels between this story and the Exodus are not accidental. God's deliverance of one man (and woman) foreshadows his deliverance of an entire nation.

The final part of the story of Abram's journey begins when he and his nephew Lot, now wealthy, leave Egypt and find that there is not enough land to support both of their families and livestock. Apparently a diplomat, Abram allows Lot to choose which land to settle in, and Lot chooses the presumably better land toward the plain of Jordan, where there are already cities, most notably Sodom and Gomorrah. Abram settles then in Canaan, which, as luck would have it, was the same place promised to his descendants by God.

Lot ends up in the thick of a battle in the region. a battle which Sodom loses, and is taken captive. Abram sends a few hundred men on a night attack of the victorious army and defeats them, taking back his nephew and some of the plunder captured from Sodom. Blessed by one of the kings, the ruler and priest of Salem (probably an early Jerusalem—see Psalm 76), the victorious Abram is also offered all of the wealth he recaptured. And here we see something of an act of faith: Abram refuses, because his prosperity will be due to no one but God. He will remain a nomad, relying only on God's open-ended promise. Oddly enough, Abram's good fortune here makes him less self-reliant; evidence that God's blessing really is with him makes him want to rely on God more. His successes have confirmed God's promise, so he will lean on that promise more heavily.

◇◇◇◇◇◇◇

Some time after this, God assures Abram more directly, appearing to him in a vision with the same nice, but perhaps kind of tired, line that he will make Abram great. Despite his successes, Abram is only getting older, and since he is still childless, all the wealth and promises of land may well seem like some kind of dark joke. In their day even more than ours, this was an all-consuming problem; all the power, the wealth, and prestige in the world would have been tradeable in an instant for a child. That is to say, Abram was a wealthy and powerful man, but one with no legacy at all—and as someone ages, doesn't legacy begin to matter more and more? The lynchpin of God's promise was painfully, embarrassingly absent.

Abram airs this grievance, and again he is promised descendants, this time of his own blood, and innumerable. To confirm the promises, God asks him to cut up some animals. This type of confirmation seems strange to the modern ear—a simple "yes" would have done nicely—but it was less odd back then. The form is that of a ritual, meticulous human preparations creating a situation with the potential for God to speak. We spoke of sacrifices at length in the Cain and Abel section, and here there's something to add: sacrifices were frequently employed to seek answers—"Shall Sparta go to war with Athens?" An animal would be killed, and some sign indicating an answer would follow. God's response to Abram is one of assurance, giving him a ritual to show, tangibly and visibly, that the promise is real.

But there's more. Behind Abram's and Sarai's inability to have a child (eleven years have elapsed since they were promised a baby) lurks a deeper question: can God really be present in this area of persistent disappointment? Most who have ever tried to conceive a child have felt the fear of infertility to some degree, even if only slightly. Abram is in the throes of this fear in its worst form, and God's stated intention of establishing a great nation through him has taken away even the comfort of stoic resignation. For eleven years, as the narrative has it, Abram has been forced to hope in a way that leaves him vulnerable to yet-worse disappointment.

In one of the cruxes of Genesis, the statement that Abram's belief "was reckoned to him as righteousness," in verse 6, expresses the truth that within the framework of God's covenant, belief—in this context, forsaking one's own viewpoint to rely wholly on God's promise—can be treated as or perhaps even becomes actual righteousness in God's eyes.

As any sufferer knows, the question of whether God is present in our moments of greatest need trumps all other questions. And if God really is present in the *worst* of life, then we can assume he's there in the good moments as well—indeed, in all of it. So our question becomes: is God still present after eleven years of unfulfilled promise? Doesn't Sarai's postmenopausal state (18:11) mean that the voice in Abram's head was false?

In answer to these questions, we uncover another layer of meaning in our cumulating reading of sacrifices: they integrate God's presence with the most seemingly God-forsaken part of life, which is death. Abram's eviscerated animals lay there, on either side of the path; can God possibly be present in the midst of them? Is he there in the most life-less parts of the world, of our lives? Abram beats away carrion birds with sticks or arms, a sick and desperate man, alone in a foreign place save an ageing family. This desperation started with his decision to follow God's call and be a nomad, and it is intensified here in a moment of total isolation. This desperation is, in part, a prerequisite for his faith.

◇◇◇◇◇◇◇◇

In the Cain and Abel story, we saw a contrast between sacrifice as earning one's way to God (Cain) and sacrifice as identification with our own powerlessness, a desperate plea for mercy. One crucial element of that story's symbolic structure is that Cain sacrifices crops, but Abel sacrifices an animal. Their respective motives, which make Abel's sacrifice pleasing to God and Cain's less so, find intimate expression in their choice of gifts. In short, Abel's sacrifice was not merely tribute to God, but it was tribute through death, the death of an animal.

Abram's sacrifice, like Abel's, is an animal one, and reading from the outward signs to the inward motives, we can identify his sacrifice as a plea for mercy precisely because *he knows the desperation of a man facing the death of both his hopes and body.* Thus even Abram's doubts and resentments against God ("for I continue childless," 15:2) are fundamentally worshipful, because they acknowledge and enact his dependence upon God. And after the sacrifice, God visits Abram in his sleep—the eight hour segment of daily life in which we most mimic the passivity of death.

And infertility is *the* symbol, par excellence, of humanity's inability to save itself.* Abram and Sarai have had the power to generate life stripped from them. Dependence, nomadism, death, doubt, grievance, sacrifice, sleep... all drive, in a marvelous symbolic interpenetration, toward God's "yes" being present in the worst of human life; indeed, being present especially in those places because he is present *as rescuer.*

---

* In addition to the Bible, the Fisher King legend, a handful of Greek myths and, in modern times, Ernest Hemingway, have employed the symbolic value of impotence to great effect.

Abram falls into sleep and darkness, presumably created, at least in part, by an intense personal identification with the death and waste and absurdity around him. Into this darkness, God speaks words of comfort to Abram's interior stream of anguish, and he gives these words an outward counterpart, the smoking pot and flaming torch in the very midst of death. God tells him, "to your descendants I give this land"—the present tense, as opposed to "I will give," marks a God faithful to his promises, recognizably faithful because he is present even in his seeming absence.

◇◇◇◇◇◇◇

That's probably the place to end, as it seems close to this story's core. But a tempting bit of speculation here would be to note that human passivity is not required for God to operate—but it *is* required for him to manifest himself to human beings. That is, he will be at work (sometimes more directly, sometimes less so) regardless of whether or not we "let" him by backing off. "Let go and let God," the popular saying, is bad theology insofar as it implies he will not work unless we let him. God's operations are his prerogative. That said, his revelation does seem to depend on our ability to perceive it, an ability which usually shrinks as our egos grow, and vice versa; this dependency stems from the fact that revelation cannot be revelation unless it is perceived.

There are three religious traditions which grow out of this story's claims about how God reveals himself—Islam, Judaism and Christianity—two of which I am not remotely qualified to comment on. But for Christianity, the idea that revelation cannot be revelation without being understood by humans, conjoined with the requirement of human passivity to understand it, produces an impasse which can only be solved by a fully passive (spiritually speaking) human, one who understands God's revelation fully and thus, in a sense, could even *be* God's revelation itself. For such a person, even crying out to God in anguish—"Why have you forsaken me?"—could open the way for the most dramatic display of God's power. Even death, the ultimate passivity, could become a precursor to resurrection.

◇◇◇◇◇◇◇

But perhaps we have veered off too far from this particular story. It is enough to say that God tends to reveal himself when humans are passive.

From his status as a nomad to his slaughtered animals to his vision in sleep, Abram enacts passivity toward God's promise, and this drives the story forward by revealing God *as God*. His actions alone guide this nomad, who has so little else to lean on. Even when Abram acts for his own preservation, as in his attempt to pass off Sarai as his sister, God still acts, above and beyond what Abram could have possibly done or anticipated. Though visible signs of God's presence, like plagues of judgment or flaming torches, seem largely lost to history, it holds true through today that human passivity provides a sort of white screen upon which God's work and agency can project. In our weakness, God's strength becomes manifest.

We all have moments when we grasp this reality in our own lives. But despite how well we may learn the lessons of passivity, our Adamic instincts toward control continually re-emerge. And so after another thirteen years of frustrated hopes, Abram will finally take the situation (rather, Sarai's servant) into his own hands and see how things work out. That is, while the covenant story occupies a "central" place in Genesis, dealing intimately with the relation between God and humans, these themes will be set aside, temporarily, while we follow Abram into an all-too-human periphery.

Ishmael and Isaac

(Genesis 16:1–18:15)

Splitting animals in half and beating birds away, becoming a nomad in the wilderness, and claiming that your eighty-something year-old wife has been promised fertility; these do seem like worthy acts of faith in hindsight. At the time, however, it would have been like an eighty-something year-old person doing those same things today—that is to say, it would have seemed deranged. To Sarai's credit, she is willing to indulge her spouse (although in those days, she may have had little choice). At least, she's willing to suspend disbelief in the "what" of God's promise—a child and a great nation—but the "how" is another matter altogether. Her suggestion to Abram to try having a child with her younger servant is not tantamount to disbelief in terms of the "what." But it does rashly claim the "how" for human agency—"God will bring this about, but maybe it's up to us to serve as the instruments."

So that's what happens: Abram "goes in" to Hagar, as the narrator tastefully puts it. She has a child, then starts feeling superior to her master, which angers an understandably envious Sarai, who promptly expels the pregnant Hagar from her house. Hagar may have been pregnant with Abram's son, but he stands by, refusing to defend her. This result is a flatly horrible one. The exile would have been a death sentence.

Despite these results, our own efforts to control things—to take the "how" into our own hands—usually come off better than this. High salaries, professional acclaim, and the respect of others often, admittedly, result from a strong sense of responsibility and need to control things. So when Abram and Sarai take things into their own hands, the lesson isn't some trite moralism about how disaster ensues from misguided initiatives. Rather, the plight of Hagar makes clear, or explicates, the internal, spiritual problems of our impulse to control the "how" of our lives. Since that impulse is so universally human, first Sarai, and then Abram, are our two entries into the story; we identify primarily with them.

◇◇◇◇◇◇◇◇

Certain parallels to the Garden of Eden become apparent: rather than waiting in dependence on God, the people in both stories take things into their own hands. Doubt—"Does God really have my best interests in mind?"—leads to the woman, Sarai/Eve, suggesting a human usurpation of God's work. The male, Adam/Abram, takes the suggestion (though it is no more Sarai's fault than his), division and blame-shifting follow, and infighting among the children of the next generation suggests a "hereditary" dimension to sin.

There is more we could say here about these similarities, but the parallel established can, by placing the two stories side-by-side, also illuminate their contrasts. The main difference is that Abram's and Sarai's fault here occurs within the framework of God's covenant. And though he will find Hagar in the wilderness and thus comfort the victim, God does not punish Abram and Sarai. His choice of them, as well as his plan to make a nation out of them, is irrevocable—there is no "if you do X and Y and Z," not even a "let go and let God," attached. Again, the covenant is asymmetrical, and God's promise exceeds the human response to it. This lapse occurs within the framework of God's plan of redemption.

Moving back for a moment to Sarai, she overestimates both Hagar's devotion to her and her own magnanimity. She very kindly allows her husband to start having sex with her servant, "taking one for the team" and generously placing her interests in a backseat to Abram's supposed destiny. The problem is that Hagar isn't as resilient to egotism as she should be, and Sarai will not prove as resistant to jealousy as she expects. Though she is a pragmatist when it comes to figuring out the "how" of God's plan, Sarai is very much an optimist when it comes to human nature. As a few of these stories suggest, and as common sense bears out, an excessive need to be in control of things is often informed by an unrealistically high view of one's capabilities, or of human capabilities in general.

To return to the Eden comparison/contrast (and start on something of a rabbit trail), this is the first time in Genesis we see master-servant relations up close. The Cain and Abel rivalry, Adam's and Eve's blame-shifting, and Abram's and Lot's tensions were all, in some sense, disagreements among equals. Here we see a relationship among unequals—one a master with almost all of the power and a corresponding responsibility to use it properly; the other a servant, with a responsibility to obey so long as the master's treatment isn't egregious.

With humanity's desire to be like God revealed in Genesis, a number of problems in relationships of unequal power emerge. First, if humans constantly attempt to usurp God's place, then of course they are willing (and actively desire) to usurp other humans' places, too. If Hagar were perfectly comfortable in her place (taking the author's moral worldview, not ours, into account), then Sarai's delegating her authority to produce an offspring to Hagar may have, ostensibly, produced less friction. With both humans now on the same plane, however—and with each desiring total mastery or dominion—*delegation* tends toward *substitution*: more power for you means less for me. And so Hagar becomes proud when she bears Abram his first child in his life and, of equal importance, a child after eleven years of waiting on God's promise to be fulfilled. Her ego necessarily conflicts with Sarai's, and strife ensues.

There's a certain literary justice here, too: Sarai infringes upon divine providence, and Hagar's contempt infringes upon Sarai's status as Abram's wife. Her sin against Sarai is simultaneously Sarai's, because it is Adam's and, therefore, humanity's. Master and servant are guilty in the same way; both act for self-advancement, and they are equal in their unity with Adam. And in pulling the universal man into the story, we as readers are immediately implicated as well. Through Adam, we identify first with Sarai, and then with Hagar.

In yet another sophisticated turn in the narrative, Sarai's banishment of Hagar functions as an obvious denial of the brute fact that this was, from the start, her idea. She is punishing Hagar for pride, something to which almost anyone in her situation would be susceptible. The fact that she lacked the foresight to realize that Hagar would become arrogant is no excuse; instead, it springs from the same optimism which lies at the center of her denial. So she reprises Adam's Fall in yet another way:

trying to skirt the reality that she is fallen. Abram, for his part, tells Sarai that she "is in your power; do to her as you please"—an attempt to skirt his own responsibility by partitioning the problem away. If he falls back on the (mistaken) idea that he owes Hagar nothing because she's Sarai's responsibility, it begins to look pretty similar to Adam's "the woman made me do it" brand of defensiveness.[*]

◇◇◇◇◇◇◇◇

In a final parallel to the Eden story, someone is driven out of her home for the sin of pride, for wanting to usurp someone else's power, dignity, etc. Unfortunately, this person is no longer necessarily the most guilty, as with Adam and Eve, but instead the most vulnerable. We saw the post-Edenic problem of a servant failing to be humble earlier; here we see the problem of a master failing to be gracious.[†] In any human hierarchy of power, sin which is shared between someone higher up and someone lower down will tend to devolve, as people scapegoat those less powerful than they, until the blame rests almost entirely on the least powerful person's shoulders. From offensive coordinators in football being scapegoated by head coaches to employees taking the fall for their bosses, this distinctly post-Edenic transmission of guilt down the metaphorical ladder is readily observable. Power gives the ego a tool with which to build itself up, and since one crucial way of ego-building is the denial of one's guilt via blame-shifting, it seems sadly inevitable that the vulnerable are often scapegoated. Thus Abram foists the problem upon his wife, and his wife promptly blames Hagar and banishes her. Paradoxically, the sin of exploitation *and* the denial of one's sinfulness are sometimes two united faces of the same impulse.[‡]

And yet Sarai is the one with whom we're called to identify. We see ourselves in her, ideally, in a way she couldn't see herself in Hagar. For us as an audience, this story's moral imperative—indeed, the reading for

---

[*] William Faulkner's short story "Delta Autumn," from his novel *Go Down Moses*, perfectly illustrates this desire to compartmentalize responsibility—and thus guilt—by making it someone else's problem.

[†] The preservation of the text's "master-servant" language here is merely to stay close to the story; replace with "politician-citizen," "parent-child," or any other relationship characterized by asymmetric power, and the ideas remain descriptive.

[‡] In Christian theology, this is one reason why confession *is itself* an act of repentance, and why it must always be emphasized over the attempt to merely change one's habits—denial, and the pride it promotes, are the root problems.

which it calls—comes down to "identify with Sarai, empathize. Her sin is yours."

Our problem is that we prefer identifying with stronger, more virtuous and respectable characters. We can easily see ourselves as Noahs, for instance, trusting God in the midst of the gale. But a passed-out and naked Noah is less often identified with. Multiple characters give us, as readers, our choice of whom we will identify with. And we will always tend to prefer characters who resonate with the good parts of ourselves, the ones we want to think about, over the characters who mirror back our bad traits.

This is another place where the story and its interpretation collide. Sarai shares our problem of identification, and this becomes the beginning, in Genesis, of favoritism. Hagar's pride does, perhaps, remind Sarai of her own Adamic pride—but rather than sympathizing with her, Sarai pushes her away. Hagar is a living, painful reminder not only of Sarai's infertility but also of her human reaction to it, which is to assert her agency. Since Sarai shares Hagar's sin, yet doesn't want to face it, Hagar is banished. And later, after Hagar is back in the house and both children are born, Sarai sees them playing with each other and banishes Ishmael. Neither he nor his mother can be too close to Sarai; she must keep them compartmentalized, and when those lines are blurred, a more dramatic break becomes necessary for her.

We will see plenty more favoritism in the stories of Jacob and Esau, Leah and Rachel, and Joseph and his brothers. For now, we can note that human favoritism involves preferring that which gives our fragile egos assurance over that which leads to self-doubt. Building off of the insights of the Eden story and that of Cain and Abel, we can see that this human favoritism is, biblically speaking, damaging. It aids the Adamic projects of self-justification and the refusal to believe that *I'm* at fault. Moreover, favoritism exposes one way we fall out of touch with reality: our delusions almost always err on the side of making ourselves look better than we are. Meaning, we identify selectively, emphasizing similarities which make us think well of ourselves, and avoiding those similarities which make us think worse of ourselves.

This is one reason why some of the best dark stories—including biblical ones—work: they force the audience to identify with a villain (Ivan in *The Brothers Karamazov*, Tony in *The Sopranos*), usually someone with enough good to draw in empathy, and enough bad to shed light on the audience's own moral ambiguities. Stories which push this agenda correct our Adamic pride, and they may even lead us toward self-awareness and confession.

◇◇◇◇◇◇◇◇

Another place where the layers of meaning in Genesis coincide especially well is in the theme of *divine* favoritism. Divine favoritism simply means that God will correct our tendencies to identify with strength and scorn weakness not merely in the Bible's stories, but also in the operation of his providence. That is, God will often express preference for the *least*; he will actively choose those who are unfit or unworthy in human terms. In Exodus, a murderer is chosen to be lawgiver, and a man with a speech impediment is chosen to champion the Israelites' cause against the world's most powerful ruler. When a prophet visits an uneducated shepherd in the book of Samuel, telling him one of his sons will be king, the only son not invited to the interview—because his father thinks him totally unfit for the job—is chosen. Divine favoritism corrects ours by choosing the least, whether in stature or birth order or even moral conduct (Rahab or, for Christians, M. Magdalene and Zacchaeus).

In this story, God is impartial. Again, since God's promise supersedes Abram's and Sarai's response to it, he remains wholly faithful to them, and later, he even salves Abram's conscience about banishing Hagar and Ishmael (a second time) for the sake of domestic peace. Which isn't to say that the victim of banishment, the mostly powerless Hagar, is left out of his favor. In a way, she too is chosen by him.

We observed earlier that human passivity, the removal of control, and the death of Adamic ambition are not required for God to work so much as to *see* God working. Hagar's journey into the wilderness reminds us not only of Adam's and Eve's banishment, but also it brings to mind Abram's own earlier journey. We again see the nomad reduced (etymologically, "led back") to a state of dependence upon God.[*] It is no mistake that biblical outcasts tend to have the keenest abilities to recognize God.

So Hagar sees "the angel of the Lord" at a spring en route to Shur, presumably a town to which she is headed for refuge. The images here layer

---

[*] See too Joseph, the Sinai wandering told in Numbers, David, Elisha, and Jesus of Nazareth's invocation of the Jewish "nomad" tradition: "the son of man has no place to lay his head." For a modern example, see Faulkner's "Old Man" story within *If I Forget Thee, Jerusalem* (alternately, *Wild Palms*) or Tolstoy's "Father Sergius."

nicely: a spring in the desert being a natural refuge as well as a stroke of good fortune for someone looking, in religious terms, for the presence of God *as Creator*, the one who carved out a space, between the waters of chaos, in which humans could dwell. This natural act of creation points toward God's role as rescuer, someone who not only creates the world for the good of his creatures but also intervenes in it on their behalf. The angel tells her to name her child Ishmael, meaning "God hears." This hearing builds upon his role as Creator of humans, and therefore someone concerned with the *whole* of humanity; even a victim of and refugee from God's chosen family will be heard by him. He is present in the dark side of history, present with its victims, in addition to his special presence with Abram and Sarai and Isaac. And God will make of Ishmael a great nation, too—which serves as an important reminder, at this point in the story, that God's special favor for Abram does not exclude his work with the whole of humanity. When Hagar calls God a "God of seeing," it seems to imply that God sees her with compassion and thus, as a result, allows himself to be seen, active and working, by her.

◇◇◇◇◇◇◇◇

A few loose ends for this section remain. God appears to Abram again, thirteen years after Ishmael's birth, to reaffirm his covenant, albeit with a couple of new twists. First, he receives a new name, Abraham, meaning "the Father is exalted" and "father of a multitude," a name not based on Abram himself, but rather his identity *as chosen*, as recipient of the God's promise. Likewise, Sarai becomes "Sarah," or "princess," which also points to God's promise.

The latter, however, is a bit ironic—renaming an extremely old woman "princess" feels a bit like a cruel joke. Sarah's bitter, acidic laughter when God tells her that she'll have a son is completely understandable. There is a tension here between God's calling Abraham a father of a multitude and the fact that he is, unfortunately, not one. And the same applies to our eighty-six year-old princess. The tension is absurd, in strictly human terms. Later, however, once Isaac is born, he is named "laughter," not in the sense of bitterness but of joy. Since the story here links Sarah's two different types of laughter, how those two moments of laughter relate to each other is worth considering.

For the first, bitter laughter, imagine an eighty year-old Des Moines city councilman who is promised by an over-energetic pastor that God will one day make him President. His laughter would be a mockery of that hope, laughing at it because it is absurd and unthinkable. On the off-chance he becomes President, he may look back at the strange sequence of events that led to such an improbable outcome and laugh to himself—"No idea how *that* happened." Both laughters occur in the face of an absurdity. The first is resigned to the impossibility of something good happening, and the second, retrospectively, wonders at how an impossible blessing actually did come to pass.

Laughter is an elusive human gesture. It is difficult to figure out when and how and why it happens, so that is probably the most we can say, for now, concerning Sarah's reaction. But the transition from resigned laughter to laughter at one's implausible good fortune points toward God's presence in the impossible and absurd. Additionally, some interpret the name "Isaac" as meaning "he laughs," in which case his very name expresses God's presence in impossibility, presence within both the pain of doubting a promise and the joy over its improbable fulfillment. This idea of hoping in the midst of hopelessness will reach a climax when God later asks Abraham to sacrifice his son.

◇◇◇◇◇◇◇◇

Two other loose ends before we move on: first, God visits Abraham in the form of three people. This "theophany," or manifestation of God, has been exhaustively glossed by Christian theology, particularly in its development of Trinitarian doctrine. Sticking to the story here, however, it is simply one of many manifestations of God. If anything, it recalls the Garden of Eden story most nearly, where God walks among humans—another physical, embodied manifestation of his presence. It's not a stretch to say that this may be the moment Sarah conceives (v 10), implying that God's direct visitation is required to produce life out of barrenness.

We remember that Adam's original mandate was to "fill the earth and subdue it" (1:28). Abraham could not fill the earth, and neither could Sarah; they were dependent upon God for fertility. As noted earlier, fertility is a symbol of potency in general, the ability of humans to create and give things life—to keep our species alive. It is fitting then that Abraham, a nomad dependent upon God, would also be dependent on him for the ability to procreate. But what about Abraham's children? Must everyone be infertile to highlight their dependence upon God for life?

This question leads to a second loose end, God's amendment of the covenant to require circumcision. To me, this seems like a visceral, embodied mark to remind us that humanity's ability to reproduce is subject to God. This is, admittedly, a pretty strange reading, and meditations on the meaning of circumcision from Jewish rabbinic sources would certainly elucidate its meaning in a more valuable way.

Wrapping up this section, Isaac, the first of Abraham's promised nation, will be marked by dependence upon God. This dependence will help Isaac, and the nation descended from him, to recognize God's presence as rescuer. Dependence does, in some sense, require weakness and humility, and God's special preference for the weak will inform Israel's identity every step of the way as a corrective to our human tendency to seek identity in things which seem strong and self-sufficient. God's choice of the weak, because it comes in the least expected place, will imply a preference for the whole; let us not forget that Israel is best represented, for example, by an underqualified shepherd-king named David.

As readers, several of the stories in Genesis will force us to identify with the least, the outcasts. When have you been totally helpless? How did it feel? It is difficult, and sometimes impossible, to force ourselves into re-calling that flash of painful memory, that frozen instant when we felt small, weak, and utterly vulnerable. But it is often through such moments, in the midst of our doubt and inability, that God's goodness becomes most clear. Even Sarah denied the fact that she laughed at God's promise. While memories of our own weakness and unbelief may be unreliable at best, we can nevertheless identify with her denial. In fact, our reluctance to face the sometimes disheartening similarities between ourselves and the characters of Genesis means that there will always be more of that elusive Adamic self to discover in the text.

Sodom and Gomorrah

(Genesis 18:16-19:29)

As Abraham's three visitors—possibly two of them angels and one of them an appearance of God—leave, Abraham escorts them partway, likely out of politeness, to "set them on their way," as the text reads. In the last chapter, we skipped ahead a bit to Isaac's birth. The correct order of events has the visit to Abraham followed immediately by the destruction of Sodom and Gomorrah—only after which do we read of the birth of Isaac.

Sometimes biblical stories employ the literary device of framing, where one story is interrupted by another, thus forming a metaphorical "frame." In this case, Sodom's and Gomorrah's destruction is placed squarely in the middle of the main narrative stream, which is Abraham and his family, serving as a literary interjection between Isaac's conception and his birth. Often, the framing story and the "framed" story comment on and help interpret each other, and this seems to be the case here. In fact, such a reading of Sodom and Gomorrah is supported by the narrative link between God's visit to Abraham and his subsequent destruction of the cities—they occur back-to-back and on the same visit to creation by the same angels. How the two stories may comment on each other is an interesting question and, at this point, one without a clear answer.

Judgment and deliverance had meanings at this time in Jewish history that were different from how they are understood by Christians today. For example, Abraham's righteousness (15:6) would not have directly implied a cosmic verdict of salvation. The deliverance was less other-worldly, primarily understood as God's blessing Abraham with children, a nation descended from him, and a legacy. Divine judgment, in the Hebrew Scriptures, similarly occurs in terms that are often more this-worldly than we might generally think: when God judges Israel, they are exiled; when nations around Israel are judged by God, some political setback usually results—a lost battle or the death of a king. The judgment of Sodom and Gomorrah here may well be, in Christian terms, a cosmic consignment to hell, or something like it. For the story, however, it primarily signifies physical death and political destruction.

In the search for a link between the main narrative of Abraham and Sodom's destruction, the first verse which jumps out is God's internal debate about whether or not to allow Abraham to witness his judgment:

> *"'Shall I hide from Abraham what I am about to do, seeing that Abraham shall become a great and mighty nation, and all the nations of the earth shall be blessed in him?'" (v 17-18)*

There is an argument against allowing Abraham to witness this destruction, and it's difficult to pin down exactly what God's reasoning is here. To take an admitted guess, perhaps God's judgment should occur separately from his salvation: since Abraham *shall* (is certainly destined to) become a great nation, is there any point in his witnessing God's judgment? He knows God's favor and promise well; perhaps he should not have to be there to watch what happens to those who have incurred God's wrath. But God does find a reason to let Abraham see what is going to happen:

> *"'No, for I have chosen him, that he may charge his children and his household after him to keep the way of the Lord by doing righteousness and justice; so that the Lord may bring about for Abraham what he has promised to him.'" (v 19)*

This second sentiment suggests that Abraham does need to see God's concern for justice and morality, because he will be asked to teach his family to "keep the way of the Lord;" which is a requirement, or condition, for God to fulfill his promise. Here we see a tension between the God of unconditional promise and the God who must, by his nature, cleanse evil and exalt goodness. The text's exploration of this tension is sophisticated for such an early point in Hebrew literature. God's promise, on the one hand, is irrevocable, but on the other, it seems conditional. It even appears that the latter concern wins out—God "contradicts" his former sentiment and decides to show Abraham the coming destruction.*

Although the second sentiment implies that God's promise depends upon Abraham and his descendants acting righteous and just, it also implies that God will bring this obedience about. And one of the ways God brings this about is by showing Abraham divine justice.

God's justice will be on behalf of history's victims, as he has heard an "outcry" against the two cities. Although the two verses cited above suggest that God knows he will destroy them, for some reason an angelic scouting mission is needed to determine whether it really is as bad as it seems. This is strange, and seemingly without reason, but often it is these strange places, the sticking points in the narrative, which call for our attention. God hearing the "outcry" against the cities recalls Ishmael's name, "God hears." And when God hears, he responds, whether by sending an angel to Hagar and promising her many descendants or by sending angels to Sodom and Gomorrah with quite different intentions. He is a God of mission, going out into the human world and human history—a God of response.

◇◇◇◇◇◇◇◇

Abraham, as the beneficiary of God's promise, is familiar with his grace. Abraham's election by God places him in a position to ask, paraphrasing, "What if destroying those wicked cities means destroying an innocent person, too? Surely it's not worth taking fifty innocent lives." We remember the words of a later Jewish teacher, telling the story of farmhands who wanted to pull up some weeds in a field: "'No; for in gathering the weeds you would uproot the wheat along with them'" (Mt 13:29). The (relatively) innocent people and the guilty ones may be in those cities together, and one group cannot be destroyed without destroying the other.

Abraham is able to intercede for the people of Sodom and Gomorrah because he knows his own dependence upon God's mercy: "It's not worth taking fifty innocent lives," God agrees. "But what about forty-five," Abraham asks, pushing the envelope in a rather annoying and hair-splitting, yet generous and well-intentioned, way. God agrees to

---

* These words are in quotation marks because, properly speaking, God does not contradict himself and does not have divergent wills. And yet, as Augustine noted in his *De Trinitate*, some language used to speak about God, though philosophically improper, can still be a valid mode of expression.

spare Sodom on account of forty-five, and then forty, thirty, twenty, and finally ten, as Abraham keeps pushing the line. He is perhaps exhibiting an appropriate response to grace: Abraham feels naturally appreciative for how God has blessed him and wants to extend that favor to others.

Unfortunately, when the angels visit Sodom to see if the "outcry" really is as great as they've heard, a mob composed of every single male in the city attempts to rape them. Lot, Abraham's nephew and the angels' host, tries to protect his visitors. He goes so far as to attempt to sacrifice his children, two virgin daughters, offering them in place of the two angelic visitors. The mob gets angry with *him*—still considered a foreigner despite having lived there for quite a while—and decides that he will do in his visitors' stead. The angels save Lot, bringing him inside in some vaguely miraculous way and blinding the mob, presumably so it couldn't force its way in. Afterward, fire and brimstone rain down as Lot, his family, and the angels flee.

It is a bizarre story, and the destruction of the cities is undeniably tragic—although less tragic, perhaps, than the ongoing atrocities of a city in which everyone was prepared to rape foreigners. In moral terms, God's judgment here is just. Whereas the flood story involved universal judgment of the whole world, this judgment is local and particular. He destroys two cities, and he would have spared them if even ten innocent people were living there. If God's judgment here still seems overly vindictive, it's worth noting that many nations have entered wars against abusive governments, knowing the removal of such governments would entail (far) more than ten non-complicit people dying. Practically speaking, the death of relatively innocent people to destroy an abusive government (think American soldiers in WWII) can be a sad, but pragmatic, necessity.

The fire and brimstone are genuinely sensational, the destruction massive. The story was used by later Israelite religion as a dark and dramatic illustration of God's power over human nations; in later Christianity, it factored into stories of hell and apocalypse. Through God's judgment, we see the horror of a human culture commensurate to it, and like rubberneckers on an interstate, we stare in awe.

◇◇◇◇◇◇◇◇

God is just, and he works to remove evil. Admittedly, the grace he shows Abraham and Sarah stands in tension to his punishment of Sodom and

Gomorrah, but again, such punishment is on behalf of victims. And although Lot's behavior here is morally ambiguous at best, he is saved on account of Abraham. Abraham's intercession for ten righteous people may have ended in futility, but his kinship to Lot is enough for God to spare his nephew.

How does all of this relate to the birth of Isaac? We recall God's reason for involving Abraham in the first place: "'For I have chosen him, that he may charge his children and his household after him to keep the way of the Lord by doing righteousness and justice, so that the Lord may bring about for Abraham what he has promised to him.'" The Sodom and Gomorrah event occurs immediately after the final, definitive promise of a son. Abraham's future is at last before him, and the nation he was promised is underway. But that nation will be asked to keep God's law as part of the covenant with him. Though this covenant will still be asymmetrical and will endure, as God promised Abraham, obedience will be required to remain in good standing with God. His judgments will still be for the sake of sin's victims—which, by the time of the prophets, are often understood as the Israelites themselves.

God's promise and judgment will be mingled in complex, strange, and often bizarre ways (for *really* bizarre, see God's attempt to kill Moses in Ex 4), and Abraham's vision of this judgmental side of God will help him both to "'charge his children and his household to keep the way of the Lord'" and to see God's grace set in sharp relief. God's destruction will be understood, at the outset, as justice on behalf of victims. And his justice will, as in the forcible rescue of Lot, sometimes spare someone because of her or his relation to the object of his covenant. Furthermore, those chosen by God will sometimes, like Abraham or later Moses (see Ex 32:10, 14), be in a position to make an appeal to God on behalf of others. His judgment will both express his will for humans to live in health and harmony, while simultaneously revealing his grace to be grace—something which arrives in spite of what merit might suggest, and something which is startling by juxtaposition against the backdrop of a very real, true, and effective moral law. The tension between irrevocable promise and the necessity of obedience will not end here; it's a recurrent theme throughout the Hebrew Scriptures and in the three world religions which have sprung from them.

The reason for God's angelic scouting-mission remains elusive, only partially explainable in terms of God's response to the cries of victims and his desire to be present in human suffering. The angels do not find ten righteous men, nor, presumably, even one. But they do end up saving Lot and his family for the sake of Abraham, and perhaps, too, because they were guests under his roof. When the angels later tell Lot to leave, he hesitates. So they forcibly grab him and make him leave the city to escape the impending fire and brimstone. The story does, despite its bleakness, end in rescue—rescue based not on heeding the angels' instructions or on exemplary conduct, but on Lot's kinship to Abraham. Again, regardless of what he deserved, Lot is rescued on account of God's promise to Abraham.

◇◇◇◇◇◇◇◇

Continuing to tie up loose ends, Lot's wife is turned into a pillar of salt when she looks backward as they flee. Some suggest that this is a legend to explain the strange salt formations in that part of the Near East, and that sounds valid. But there may be more to it, a point being made which fits in with the rest of the story's symbols and meanings. I find such a meaning indecipherable, and would only hazard a guess that concern for the city somehow implicated Lot's wife in nostalgia for the judged city, and this paralyzing nostalgia, or inability to move on from the city, is symbolized by her transformation to an immobile pillar of salt.

◇◇◇◇◇◇◇◇

"'I have chosen him, that he may charge his children and his household after him to keep the way of the Lord by doing righteousness and justice; so that the Lord may bring about for Abraham what he has promised to him.'"

Abraham witnesses the Lord's destruction here to see his justice, and God's concern for victims is a valuable lesson, following Abraham's earlier disavowal of Hagar. We noted earlier that in Genesis, procreation can be a potent field for human self-justification and that sex drive, even when someone doesn't consciously want children, still derives from an inbuilt genetic instinct to reproduce. Abraham's "going in" to Hagar represented an attempt to take God's promise of children into his own hands. Additionally, we can see that one reason the Judeo-Christian tradition sees "lust" as a sin is that it results from a selfish use of sex drive, trying to carry on reproduction (again, even if only implicitly) without caring for the other person. Such was Abraham's treatment of Hagar, using her for *his and Sarah's* children. Hagar, at first proud because she conceived instead of Sarah, soon realized her true status, and Abraham's true feelings, when he stood by as Sarah banished her (pregnant) to the wilderness.

A darker, more twisted and horrible version of Abraham's sin was attempted at Sodom—rape is the most extreme case of using another person to satisfy one's own self-perpetuating libido, and we even see Lot's daughters, the last remnant of Sodom, use their father in the same way after they escape. Now that God's action in history has narrowed primarily to a family, that of Abraham, sex is the currency of self-justification, and it becomes impossible to ever fully separate sex from power. God was concerned with Hagar and appeared to her in the desert, but here he destroys the victimizers. And not only does untethered, unrestrained self-reliance via libido produce victims, but also, in a way, it competes with God. In Abraham's case and Israel's (circumcision), God will be recognized as the one to whom humans owe everything: their existence and continuation. And so perhaps God chooses not to hide his judgment from Abraham not only because Abraham must "'charge his children and his household to keep the way of the Lord,'" but also for the reason that God will make Abraham into a nation, period. Israel must understand that procreation comes from God, and sex, as the currency of family, must be used accordingly.

If all of this sounds moralistic, it maybe is—but no more so than the story itself here. And if the sex stuff seems strange, it probably is. But losing the sexual focus risks severing this account's links to the Hagar story, its contrast to Babel (justification by power there, by sex here), its commentary on Lot's daughters, and some of the light it will shed on a couple of strange episodes later, in the stories of Tamar and Potiphar's wife.

◇◇◇◇◇◇◇◇

For now, however, we are left with Abraham expecting, finally, the promised son next spring, as well as quite a bit to ponder after being shown God's judgmental side. "No, for I have chosen him..." As readers, God presents to us this strange episode in the narrative as a consequence of presenting it to Abraham. It is a sensational and grotesque story, with fewer immediate takeaways or obvious meanings than some of the others. Or maybe it is just less decipherable to the contemporary ear. Nonetheless, it is given to us to witness, perhaps for reasons similar to why it was given to Abraham: to reveal God's power and justice alongside his deliverance. However little sense it may make to a modern ear, or however unpalatable it may seem, "fire and brimstone" is what the angel lets us see; it is not withheld. And when attempts to explain this episode fail, we might remember that the angel did not explain it to Abraham either, but merely chose not to hide it from him. And to us, even the biblical images which seem to connect less than others still work, somehow, for good, even if as strange and primal images which shock us, and thereby draw us out of ourselves.

The Sacrifice of Isaac

(Genesis 22:1-19)

This story begins with God calling Abraham, no longer with promise and covenant, but with command. He tests Abraham, as the text puts it, by ordering him to take his son a few days' journey from home, kill him, and then burn him as a sacrifice. Later, just as Abraham is raising his knife to kill his son, God tells him to stop; he was just making sure Abraham feared him (a word which here means something between our modern "fear" and "respect"). God gives him a ram to sacrifice instead.

As we look back on this story, a common misreading is viewing Abraham simply as an impressive man of faith. He certainly *was* a man of faith, and that faith was impressive, but there is much more to it. We cannot pass over the horror of Abraham actually deciding to kill his son—prepared to commit a brutal act.

In 2003, a Texas woman killed her eight and six year-old children by bludgeoning them with a rock, and she attempted to kill her 15-month old son, Aaron, who sustained permanent injury. She decided to kill them—and was reportedly calm when she dialed 911 to report their deaths—because God told her to. It was a divine command, and she obeyed. Far from being considered a "woman of faith," she was acquitted on account of insanity, because—the defense's argument ran—no one could ever kill their children on account of a *real* divine command. She must have been hallucinating, plagued by psychosis.

Abraham was prepared to do the same thing for the same reason, and his case is, ethically speaking, scarcely more defensible than hers. In order to see him as a true person of faith, we must first see him as a filicidal monster. So the first thing which jumps out from the story, if we don't gloss over it, is the horror of Abraham's decision to kill his son. He cannot be a person of faith or obedience without having been absolutely prepared to murder Isaac. If we want to call it sacrifice, rather than murder... then the infanticidal religious nuts of the world deserve the same description. Can something be truly pious if it violates one of the central principles of morality of the world, *do not kill anyone, and certainly not your children*?

Assuming Abraham was told to do this by God, God looks exceedingly capricious and cruel—this is the second thing which stands out. Afterward, the angel tells Abraham, "Do not lay your hand on the boy... for now I know that you fear God." As a test of Abraham's love, this is absurdity. Consider a woman who asks her husband for permission to cheat on him: "I'm doing it no matter what, whether you approve or not." When the husband, in extreme anguish, replies that she can go ahead and do it and he won't divorce her, she replies, "I didn't really want to—just wanted to make sure you loved me unconditionally." This, at first glance, is similar to what God is doing to Abraham, something deeply insecure and petulant. The "test" here is cruel.

This story pushes on the absolute limits of what we may believe of God and of Abraham, and that is one reason why it has consistently been considered one of the finest literary masterpieces of Genesis and perhaps of the entire Hebrew Scriptures. But we cannot see its beauty without allowing its horror to present itself—what if you heard voices in your head, claiming to be God, and telling you to kill *your* child? Or parent, sibling, or spouse, as the case may be? We must identify with Abraham here and imagine his anguish. The story's horror demands to be its starting-point.

◇◇◇◇◇◇◇◇

This account represents the climax of Abraham's life as it is recorded in Genesis, the moment at which his covenant of dependence on God, which up until now has benefitted him, suddenly turns against him and requires him to destroy himself (who could remain sane, who could live with herself after killing a child?), his son, his marriage (how could Sarah ever understand?), and finally, all the promises and blessings of God, which have centered around Abraham being given descendants who will become a nation. It will make Abraham worse off than he ever was without God; in Ur in his early life, he at least didn't have the pain of killing a child on his conscience. We as readers want to look away, but we cannot, because we are implicated both in Abraham's decision to kill his son *and*—only by virtue of that first identification—in God's deliverance of him at the story's end.

To understand our identification with Abraham, we must go back to the earlier stories which, while stories in their own right, also anticipate this one. First, there is Adam, who represents all of us and refuses to live as a creature, who brings sin into the world. Rather than accepting his guilt, he tries to blame it on Eve—"The woman told me to!" Then their children, Cain and Abel, show sin's infiltration into human relationships, and they reveal sin to be, in large part, our misguided initiative in tying ourselves back to God. Abel, as someone whom God chooses over Cain, becomes a living reproach to his brother, prompting his brother to kill him. Thus, the murderous bent of Adam's blame-shifting is revealed: trying to make someone else bear our guilt is a murderous impulse, because we can only build ourselves up, in our own eyes, by putting others down. The tendency to put others down reaches its climax in Cain's murder, and the effects of sin reach even into the family.

Cain's anger over his guilt before God leads him to actually become guilty. This first murder occurs in a sibling context for the simple reason that human competition's most fundamental example is sibling rivalry: two equals cannot tolerate being equals, and the parents' (or God's) preference of one will infuriate the other, and lead him to over-compensate by acting out against his brother or sister. All this indicates that in a post-Edenic world in which humans are in conflict from day one ("the woman made me!"), human self-justification requires a victim.

The story of Cain and Abel also introduces the notion of sin as something that is inherited. The two sons repeat and dramatize their parents' wrongdoing; in a sense Adam and Eve are responsible for what happens. Any parent who has had a child do poorly in school, develop an addiction, bully others, or even get a bad report card knows this feeling well—"What did I do wrong?"

The ideas of inherited sin and victimizing self-justification are important here, as is the tension between sacrifice as self-renunciation and sacrifice as a legalistic way to earn God's favor that we see so clearly in the story of Cain and Abel. The command to sacrifice a son pulls from each of these ideas: the responsibility for one's child, the need for a victim, and the extreme self-renunciation inherent in the willingness, however conflicted, to commit infanticide. In the first case, Abraham's denial of responsibility for Hagar, and the banishment to the wilderness of his *other* son, must have weighed heavy on his mind during the agonizing three-day journey to Moriah. And whatever normal, human angers, resentments, blame-shiftings or rivalries he must have felt were almost murderous, at least from a later perspective (Jesus of Nazareth placed anger on the ethical level of murder, Mt 5:22). The point here is merely that as a child of Adam, Abraham carries the sin of Cain within himself. And so when he decides to kill his son he not only *becomes* guilty of filicide, he also comes face-to-face with the dark side of his nature—both his tendency to victimize others (Hagar, 16:6), and his pride, i.e., his self-image as someone who does not kill.

◇◇◇◇◇◇◇◇

This final point, Abraham's impending ethical death, can be supported in three ways. First, we have a basic obligation to other humans, and particularly to children. Emmanuel Levinas, a Jewish philosopher, had the idea that any time someone sees a human face, the encounter contains an imperative: "thou shalt not kill me".[*] We don't need philosophy to bear this out; it resonates profoundly with experience. The face of one's child, furthermore, imposes this fundamental obligation in an especially direct, profound way. Second, Søren Kierkegaard, in his famous commentary on this story, stresses that Abraham contradicts ethics, the father's obligation to love his son.[†] As Kierkegaard puts it, either "Abraham was a murderer every minute or we stay with the paradox... "[‡] And finally, the story's symbolism suggests the same.

When Abraham and Isaac walk up the mountain, Isaac bears the instrument of his destruction, the wood which will immolate him, and Abraham carries the knife and torch, the instruments which will make him guilty of murder. In some sense, both approach God ready to sacri-

---

[*] Emmanuel Levinas, *Totality and Infinity* (Norwell, MA: Kluwer Academic, 1991).

[†] Johannes de Silentio [Søren Kierkegaard], *Fear and Trembling*, trans. Alastair Hannay (New York, NY: Penguin, 1985). I'm indebted throughout this section to Kierkegaard's central insight that there may be, in religion and especially in this story, a "teleological suspension of the ethical" which is faith.

[‡] Ibid., 95.

fice themselves—the first, though unwittingly, his life; the second, with full intention, his child, sanity, identity, and legacy.

Abraham ties up Isaac so that he cannot escape and lays him on top of the wood. As Abraham raises the knife, an angel from God tells him stop—the sacrifice is no longer required, because God knows that Abraham is willing to sacrifice Isaac. A ram, caught in a nearby thicket, is suddenly noticed; Abraham sacrifices it instead. God himself does provide the sacrifice, and in doing so, he saves Isaac from his death and Abraham from his guilt.

∞∞∞∞∞

Before we rush in to talk about God's grace, another incongruity of the story sticks out: why is the ram necessary? In other words, if the point was testing Abraham, and Abraham proved obedient, why doesn't God just tell him to go home? We cannot demand that everything in the story make sense, in part because story is necessarily mystery (as experience itself cannot be fully explained) and in part because this story tells itself as history: God could have far-reaching historical purposes beyond our comprehension. But still, it is worth thinking through.

What if God had just told Abraham, "now I know you love me—go home"? In that case, there would be no grace, only caprice and cruelty, like the couple used as an example earlier: "I didn't really want to cheat on you, just to test you to see if you'd love me even then." If that kind of testing is unworthy for humans, how much more so for God. So the "test" here was more than a whimsical instance of divine caprice. The need for Isaac to be sacrificed was not a ruse—"If I asked you to do this, would you?"—but rather something real, an *actual* requirement in addition to a test. Isaac is not spared because God was merely testing his father. He is spared because a ram is provided; "God himself will provide the lamb," as Abraham had told his son (22:8). So the ram is not incidental, but a vital part of the story.

Would Abraham have been altogether wrong if there had been no ram in the thicket? God *did* provide Isaac, so in some sense Abraham's words to his son would not have been fully a lie. And here we see most clearly the character of sacrifice as death, as dependence; Abraham is willing to obey God partly because he knows that Isaac does not belong to him, but was very clearly a gift from God.

Killing Isaac would enact Abraham's dependence upon God in an incredibly vivid way, and killing an animal, as we saw in Abraham's ritual covenant with God, also enacts dependence. There are two senses in which sacrifice enacts this dependence: first, as substitution. Sacrifice as substitution implies that God has the ability to demand one's life; properly, it belongs to him, both as creator and as judge. Animal sacrifice acknowledges this owing of life to God, and as such it honors him; as a divine requirement, it happens so that the individual may enjoy God's blessing. That is, the animal dies so that the person doing the sacrifice may better live. This substitution also implies an identification: the animal's death symbolizes a personal death before God.

The Isaac story entails both aspects: his death on behalf of Abraham because Abraham, apparently, can only remain in God's promise by choosing to kill him. Second, Abraham identifies with Isaac, empathizing in the way that only a father can. Isaac's death will be the end of Abraham's life, too. And finally, Abraham's guilt as a killer is intimately bound up with his obedience to God. Abraham was not innocent, and now he must take his sin to its most horrifying conclusion.

In view of these concerns, the sacrifice was something required by God. It was required for Abraham to make an instance of, or instantiate, his sin in the most dramatic possible way; it was required for him to recognize the necessity, in a post-Edenic world, of victims; and it was required of him to acknowledge and instantiate his state of metaphorical death before God. Even though Abraham passes God's test of obedience and "fear," some actual fulfillment of the need to sacrifice is required. The killing of the ram, since Abraham was so near to killing his son, must have been an intensely spiritual experience, full of joy, humility, and gratitude to God. But the ram cannot totally fulfill the tasks of acknowledging dependence and being granted righteousness from God. Thus this sacrifice must be provisional, and the later Jewish code requiring regular sacrifices will pick up on the provisional, or temporary, nature of each one. Although it is provisional, we see in part here the necessity of some sacrifice, and thus God's gift of the ram becomes something which saves Isaac's life.

∞∞∞∞∞∞∞

Additionally, there is a power dynamic at play, one which builds on Abraham's and Sarah's treatment of Hagar. This is not sibling rivalry, but rather it is the power of a father over his son, who is fully dependent on him. If we place ourselves in Abraham's shoes, his son's blind trust and pliant obedience must have been one of the most excruciating parts of this episode. One literary device here is an implicit parallel of Abraham's fatherhood—leading his unknowing son to his death—to God's fatherhood, as God will lead Abraham, who does not yet know how God will deliver him, to his own ethical death. Abraham's pain could be projected onto God, who wants Abraham to live and not die. God's concern is with the victim, in this case Isaac as Abraham's victim and Abraham himself as the victim of God's command. The ram delivers both perpetrator and victim; it saves Abraham from his moral/emotional death and Isaac from his literal death. Since Abraham cannot provide any sacrifice except Isaac, God provides the ram.

Thus relations among humans, who can only elevate themselves by doing violence to others—an idea not explicitly present in this story, but still lurking in its background—can only be equalized and reconciled by God making provision for them. As the later Jewish prophets will make clear, human sin harms the Israelites themselves, their relationships to each other and their integrity as a nation. The only remedy for this is divine provision, whether in saving the nation and re-establishing it (which happens time and again) or in ignoring their sins, being patient with them. Sometimes, passing over their sins is even understood as harming God himself; for example in Hosea, where God is portrayed as the husband of a prostitute (Israel) who nonetheless remains fully committed to her.

Adam fell by neglecting to live as a human (i.e., a creature fully dependent upon God) and, instead, trying to be divine. The result of his sin was a deep sense of shame (fig leaves) which caused him to blame-shift to Eve and led, through his children, to murder. Abraham's action moves in the opposite direction: in choosing to violate ethics, he takes blame upon himself, becoming absolutely guilty; his shame in leading his (relatively) innocent son to his death is addressed directly by God. In becoming explicitly guilty and thereby recognizably dependent upon God, Abraham becomes fully human, acknowledging what he is; he moves in the opposite direction of Adam and, in humbling himself, is honored by God.

In this view, the sacrifice of the ram takes on another dimension, recalling God's slaying of an animal to provide Adam and Eve with skins to wear. The sacrifice here takes away Abraham's shame, clothing it not in his own pretension, but in God's gift. As in his change of name, Abraham will be defined neither by his obedience nor by his guilt, but by God's promise, which will remain true in the darkest ordeals. And the nation of Israel's existence will, henceforth, be defined even more sharply by its reliance upon God's murky, vague, open-ended yet wholly solid promise, as well as its absurd, counterintuitive, humanly unthinkable yet fully certain fulfillment.

"Because you have done this," God says, "by your offspring shall all the nations of the earth gain blessing for themselves." Israel will model God's providence to the world, though there's a further point that could be made. The suggestion that blessing the world will require Abraham's offspring to play the ram's part is an unavoidable one, since in this story, the ram is the agent of blessing. If Abraham's offspring may bless the world through dependence and self-sacrifice, there emerges the hope of a blessing greater than spiritual leadership—the hope that one day, a new Isaac could be a human sacrifice which is not provisional but eternal, and one which saves us both from guilt and from death.

Jacob as Son, Brother, and Husband

(Genesis 25:19-33:20)

We have finished examining two series of stories, or "cycles," in Genesis: God's relation to the world before Abraham (1:1-1:32) and God's call and blessing of Abraham (12:1-5:10). We turn now to Abraham's descendants, as they will begin multiplying into the family and nation which God has promised. This final part of the text focuses primarily on Jacob (later renamed "Israel") and his family, with the story of his son Joseph receiving disproportionate attention. It takes up roughly the final quarter of Genesis. Before the Joseph story, however, Jacob's early family life and later marriages exhibit a strong literary unity, which makes it possible to treat them as one long episode.

We are concerned here with only a few characters: Isaac, his wife Rebekah, their sons Esau and Jacob, Jacob's wives Leah and Rachel, and his clever, scheming father-in-law, named Laban. The story opens with another instance of infertility. Just as Sarah and Abraham could not have children, neither can Rebekah and Isaac. Again, their inability to reproduce will serve as a symbol of the family's dependence upon God. The nation cannot perpetuate itself, and even though later Israelites will, for the most part, be able to have children, these stories of the patriarchs will shape their imaginations, reminding them of their nation's original, miraculous origins.

Yet Isaac prays, God answers, and Rebekah conceives. If the Cain and Abel and Ishmael and Isaac stories were clues, sibling rivalry will dominate, showing yet again the zero-sum game of human ambition: more for me requires less for you. The same happens here even from the womb, where original sin is acted out through the brothers, even before birth, fighting with each other, so much so that Rebekah's pregnancy is almost unbearably painful (25:22). God tells her that the two will be in conflict, with the elder serving the younger. Perhaps this first prophecy about the fates of her two children sets Rebekah on a path toward her later favoritism.

Human favoritism, which we can again describe as identifying with the person who makes you feel better about yourself, comes into play here in a way that will eventually wreck the family. The twins develop vastly different personalities: "Esau was a skillful hunter, a man of the field, while Jacob was a quiet man, living in tents" (25:27). This description of Jacob seems like a euphemism; we can imagine that he was someone who failed to be the sort of man people at the time would have expected. Rather than becoming strong and killing animals and providing for his family, Jacob cooks and "lives in tents." There are a number of contemporary insults for this, "sissy" being the least offensive. And as we later learn, Jacob also seems to be a coward, on the run from some threat or another for almost this entire section of Genesis. He's a "mamma's boy," and she prefers him to his brother, while their father presumably is more taken with Esau's version of manliness and capability.

In addition to his cowardice—one of the most contemptible traits a person at the time could have—Jacob is far from a paragon of virtue. As he's manning the stove one day, his brother comes in from hunting. Esau is so hungry that he's about to die. Jacob, who is well-fed and content, refuses him food, preparing to watch his brother die (or possibly bluffing, though doing so convincingly). Jacob will only give his brother food if Esau relinquishes his birthright; in other words, Esau must give Jacob most of the family's inherited wealth, which traditionally went to the oldest. Jacob catches his brother at a low point and mercilessly exploits him.

In modern-day terms, imagine your brother's leg is caught in a railroad track, with an oncoming train only three minutes away. "I'll pull you out," you say, "but only if you sign this contract promising me your portion of our parents' inheritance." If male siblings then were anything like the ones I've encountered today, we imagine Jacob as a kid being pushed around, losing fights to his stronger and tougher twin, being teased. Here he finally gets his opening, and he takes it with cold brutality.

∞∞∞∞∞∞

Later, when the brothers are well into adulthood, Isaac decides to settle the family legacy, being old, frail, weak, and possibly near death. He faces a question: he has two children, and one must carry on the family name and leadership. He solves the problem, as did many families at the time, with the custom of primogeniture: the eldest son will receive the honor of family leadership along with most of the wealth. Jacob has already deprived him of the latter, but Esau will receive the father's blessing, which will give him something final and irrevocable, since it is imbued with ceremonial and religious significance. So Isaac tells Esau to prepare him a meal; it is a touching moment in which an old and infirm father asks his son to make his favorite dish before he formally gives him the family blessing. But Rebekah overhears, and driven by a mixture of favoritism and perhaps some friction with Esau's wife (26:35, 27:46), she decides to trick her now-blind husband into blessing the wrong child.

It is hard to overstate how cruel this is. Again, a modern-day paraphrasing might help: your blind father likes you more than your brother and has given you most of his inheritance, but your mother and brother draft a new will giving him most of the estate, and as your father lies helpless on his hospital bed, they trick him into signing it. It's an unthinkable betrayal of a husband and father, an exploitation of a blind man, a defrauding of a brother of his rightful share of the estate, etc. And when Isaac expresses surprise that his son killed, cleaned, and cooked game in such a short amount of time, Jacob buys credibility by saying that "the Lord your God granted me success" (27:20). Misusing God's providence to manipulate a blind father—all of this really is appalling.

Isaac understands he cannot go back; the blessing, as a ceremony before God, cannot be taken away. So Esau has nothing left except his fury, and Isaac—resigned already to Jacob being his successor—blesses Jacob again, advising him to marry well and echoing his mother's advice to flee before Esau kills him. After Jacob flees, Esau tries to please his parents by taking another wife, one his parents will like more, but the damage has been done. And Jacob, simultaneously a reprehensible person *and* the object of God's promise, is on the run from his betrayed brother.

∞∞∞∞∞

As he flees toward Laban, Rebekah's brother who can shelter and protect him, Jacob dreams of a ladder from heaven to earth, with God's angels "ascending and descending on it" (28:12). Later Jews and Christians will provide profound commentary on this vision, but for now, it doesn't offer much immediate meaning. God, although he is in the heavens and transcendent, will be with the earth, and especially with Jacob and Jacob's descendants. He will be a God of mission, and his angels (signifying his operation in the world) will be a link between him and the world. That is, he will be present in history through action ("descending"), and history will glorify him ("ascending"). The world is one graced by God's work, and God is a God for humans, one who works for our good.

That is about all we can say for now, but the symbol of the ladder makes visual and explicit this truth of Genesis: the close unity between God and history. For a man scared and (one would hope) ashamed, this vision is a comforting one. Although Jacob received his father's blessing through betrayal and cold ambition, even manipulations such as these are not outside the scope of providence. God confirms the blessing after all. And we see Jacob already humbled: his first priority is no longer wealth and fame, but reconciliation, the hope that God "will give me bread to eat and clothing to wear, so that I may come again to my father's house in peace" (28:20-21). He too has become a nomad, uncertain and largely helpless; it may be the result of his sin, but he is already enacting the pattern of his grandfather, the object of God's promise.

∞∞∞∞∞

So Jacob is estranged from his family, and it is his own fault. He's on the run, and he wants reconciliation, so the story will not be complete until he meets Esau again; the story demands either a confrontation or a reconciliation. Nestled within the story of Jacob's relationship with Esau is another story, that of his search for a wife. The two stories are grouped together here because again, we have a frame structure. Jacob's courting of Leah and Rachel will comment upon his estrangement from Esau.

Part of the unity of these two stories comes from Laban, Jacob's uncle, who is someone every bit as conniving as his sister and nephew. Jacob and Laban are similar, and though Jacob comes to him for protection, Laban will outwit and use him in the same way Jacob tricked his father. As Jacob draws close to Laban's house, he meets some of Laban's shepherds getting water from a well. While talking with them, Laban's daughter Rachel arrives too, and Jacob immediately falls in love with her. After about a month of working for his uncle, Laban asks him what his wage should be, and Jacob decides he will work for the right to marry Rachel. And as the narrative says, although seven years of labor was the price, all that time "seemed to him but a few days because of the love he had for her" (29:20). They have an evening wedding, the bride comes in a veil, and Jacob sleeps with her. But when he wakes up in the morning, it's the wrong person—Laban's older, less attractive ("weak-eyed") daughter Leah. Laban justifies his trick by saying it's custom to marry the older daughter first, but after a week-long "honeymoon" with Leah, Jacob can marry Rachel immediately—in return for another seven years of work afterward.

Whereas Jacob's father Isaac was blind, and thereby blessed the wrong child, Jacob now finds himself in darkness of his own, that of his tent, in which he marries the wrong daughter. There's a certain justice here; Jacob's deception of his father is mirrored in Laban's deception of Jacob. As before, each story tends to comment on those prior to it. The original sibling rivalry of direct, religious self-justification between Cain and Abel becomes refracted into different areas of competition which share (as Genesis suggests) an ultimately spiritual root. Furthermore, the Eden story included Adam and Eve covering up with fig leaves, trying to project an image of themselves to cover up the real, vulnerable, broken people underneath. These two threads are combined in the competition over physical beauty (which Leah is constantly losing), a rivalry which continues to create friction after the marriage, when Jacob will still love Rachel more.

Speaking of Adam's and Eve's shame, imagine Leah's as she walks into the tent that night. These were humans, just like us; imagine the fear of being found out as an imposter; the desperate and tormenting hope that maybe Jacob will love her, the next morning, after the original shock; the horrible moment when Jacob reviles her the morning after. The only way she can make a man love her is by tricking him, covering up her true self. Leah's fig leaves are the darkness of the tent; by hiding her appearance, she earns a superficial love which will turn away the moment it truly recognizes her.

We all want to earn the love of other humans—and of God. Yet it does not work because it usually involves some form of pretension, putting on airs. The fig leaves hide Adam's and Eve's shame, but in hiding it, they actually reveal it, since that shame consists precisely in self-justification. And Leah, at her father's urging, uses darkness as the great equalizer to thwart her fears that she is outwardly less worthy of love than her sister. Anyone feeling inferior while being judged will put on a facade of superiority, as did in Jacob usurping Esau's birthright or Leah in stealing Rachel's husband.

We spoke earlier of physical modesty as the resistance to being known as you are. Leah here epitomizes this, covered with a veil and with the darkness of the tent. In purely human terms, the deception cannot succeed. Simply put, if one sister is prettier than another, there's nothing anyone can do about it. After Leah's honeymoon with her new husband, who spends much of the time thinking about her sister, Leah must stand by while he marries Rachel. Deception doesn't solve the problem of competition; if anything, it makes it worse.

God does address the problem in a direct way by actively choosing the "inferior" person. Leah has children before Rachel, and she has more of them. The only way to close the performance gaps in all the various arenas of human competition is to choose the lowest, the weakest. And so the unloved Leah has more children—even if her husband never much cares for her. His preference for Rachel and neglect of Leah will have consequences well into the next generation, as we'll see in the next chapter. For now, Jacob's story is not over, as he has not yet reconciled with his family.

◇◇◇◇◇◇◇◇

It's not difficult to imagine Jacob having more empathy with his blind father after this episode. Jacob can still marry Rachel, the very next week, in return for another seven years' work following upon the wedding. But his father blessed the wrong child after a willful deception, and this altered the entire course of the family (later nation) to one which ran counter to the ageing man's wishes. Given how closely the two deceptions are narratively linked, it is not a stretch to imagine that Jacob is beginning to feel remorse. He does not deserve the blessing, and he did not earn it. And perhaps there's a fear of being found out too, à la Leah the morning after: the wrong child, people may say, a usurper. Esau may well kill him. Jacob's deception victimized not only his brother, but his father as well.

We see the link between Jacob and Laban, both slippery and smart, deepen as Laban later offers Jacob livestock for payment, just as Jacob is preparing to leave. Jacob volunteers to take only the speckled animals, and Laban agrees... before removing, that night, all the speckled ones and going miles away to hide them. Rarely outwitted, Jacob finds a way (a method now biologically dubious) to make Laban's strongest animals develop speckled skin. He takes them and flees, running once again from an act of fraud.

◇◇◇◇◇◇◇◇

Being deceived by Laban the same way he deceived his father has not quite brought Jacob to his senses. He still manages to trick Laban out of his best livestock, and as Leah's marriage to Jacob has made clear, deception obscures the real person. It never succeeds in making a solid, reliable way forward because it causes our value to depend upon a high-maintenance illusion. Consequently, the gap between what Jacob has taken and what he deserves looms over his head, forcing him to run to keep his past from catching up with him.

Hollywood provides a helpful illustration here. In *Catch Me If You Can*, Leonardo DiCaprio plays Frank Abagnale, someone who has grand dreams and cons his way into becoming a pilot, a prominent doctor, and a lawyer. The gap between his title and his true self—an unqualified kid on the run—is always closing. In Jacob's case, deception really is a form of self-justification, and his deceptions bleed over into the realm of religious pretension. But just as Leah was found out in the cold light of morning, Jacob too must be "found out" in his true self, and this tension between his posturing and the self underneath, family heir and con artist, haunts and drives the narrative.

On the run, Jacob meets God himself, who wrestles with him using a human body. The two are locked in a stalemate until God miraculously dislocates Jacob's hip. It's a strange episode, and analysis here veers inevitably toward speculation. But to take a shot at it, from Jacob's struggle with Esau in the womb up through his tense meeting with Laban, Jacob has been fighting and struggling for his place in the world, to make a name for himself. In the end, this activity may be understood as striving against God, trying to wrest his promised blessing from the world using his own means. Always having to stay a step ahead, ready to flee when you're discovered, is undoubtedly exhausting. And God allows himself to be "beaten;" throughout Jacob's life, God has refrained from any miraculous, hip-touching intervention. He has not interfered in Jacob's admittedly fraudulent life. Even if Jacob's cunning and manipulation and striving were misguided, they have still worked for good, for God's providence. So Jacob does indeed prevail.

The hip-touch, however, suggests that God could intervene miraculously but hasn't—up until now. This "theophany" (appearance of God in the world) *is* the miraculous intervention, and the hip dislocation humbles Jacob. God grants that Jacob has "prevailed," but Jacob, for his part, considers himself lucky to have scraped by with his life. Even after the dislocation, Jacob holds on, demanding God's blessing. After all his scheming and ambition, Jacob knows it comes down to this one blessing, the one which cannot be earned by plotting or posturing. Isaac's blindness, for which Jacob exploited him, takes on new meaning with God's willful blindness to Jacob's lifetime of deception. Or, conversely, Jacob is finally "seen" by someone and loved for who he is—either explanation works well within the thematic space of Isaac's blessing and Leah's wedding night. It is fitting, then, that Jacob's new name, Israel, means one who wrestles with God.

◇◇◇◇◇◇◇◇

Jacob has reached a moment of self-discovery; he is mature as a character. All that remains to be resolved is one final problem: his estrangement from the brother who is a living testament against him, his twin who hates him. If Jacob had battled Esau and won (and he wouldn't have—"a quiet man, living in tents"?), there would be no need for reconciliation or justice for the victim. It would simply be a story of a smart, ambitious man and his ill-gotten gains. Yet the biblical heroes are not wicked people who steal power and escape—that sort of story is rarely considered worthy of any kind of literature. But neither are the biblical heroes righteous, disadvantaged people who prevail against all odds—although that sort of story appears often in non-biblical literature. Rather, these characters tend to be deeply flawed people who nonetheless know their dependence upon God, and grace prevails despite, or even within, their faults. So Jacob will not get off scot-free, but neither will he transform, overnight, into someone who deserves Esau's acceptance. Instead, the moment of reconciliation occurs when Jacob bows formally to Esau several times, fearing the worst... and Esau rushes to hug him; they kiss and weep. He has been caught, trapped in a situation from which there is no escape, and only there is he known fully for the first time and loved. His story has reached its climax; the darkness and blindness and fig leaves are gone, and Jacob, vulnerable and literally at his brother's mercy, finds a real acceptance which he never could have schemed for nor earned.

◇◇◇◇◇◇◇◇

One final clue to the story emerges when Jacob says that seeing his forgiving brother "is like seeing the face of God—since you have received me with such favor" (33:9). There are several layers to this statement, the first being mere excitement, happiness. But there's also Jacob's wonder at his good fortune; we could paraphrase his response to seeing God to fit this encounter: "I have seen Esau face-to-face, and yet my life is preserved." God has been the judge the whole time; since self-justifying sibling rivalry is rooted in Adamic spiritual pretensions (as with Cain and Abel), Jacob has indirectly been trying to achieve righteousness, to please God. And the link between darkness, blindness, and fig leaves reveals Leah to have been pursuing the same project, earning love through deception.

The continuing presence of these motifs reveals an element to the story that transcends Leah, Jacob, and their times and places. We too try to earn love through deception, presenting "better" versions of ourselves to family, friends, and even (especially) ourselves. Our true selves are obscured and therefore unloved.

There is hope, however, and Jacob's story models how forgiveness and the unexpected action of grace may cut through our misguided pretensions. At last, Jacob is revealed before his brother and before God, and his "yet my life is preserved" expresses the wonder of encountered, experienced grace. Parsing the Esau-God comparison more closely, we see that the similarity between seeing Esau's face and seeing God's occurs primarily because "you have received me with such favor." "Yet my life is preserved" is itself a miracle, both in Jacob's wrestling with God and in his meeting with Esau.

But the action of grace here extends beyond toleration, even beyond forgiveness; it overlooks fault *and then*, in addition, finds "such favor" with the one who does not deserve it. Reconciliation here depends upon forgiveness, and Jacob, in receiving it, finally grows into the spirit of his grandfather, Abraham, who was characterized by dependence upon the absurdity of God's provision. Here, at the end of himself, Jacob takes this providence to heart—the gap between pretension and reality finally closes. As a result, Jacob's development into a patriarch, one who relies upon God's promise, is complete.

The Joseph Story, Part One

(Genesis 37:1–37:36)

Most of us, if we had a dream about our older siblings bowing down to us, would keep that dream to ourselves. We would presumably suspect that it's likely more driven by ego than revelation. But Joseph appears to be different from you or me. He boldly tells his brothers (who already hate him) about his dream, and they decide, with a solid eleven-man consensus, that they cannot live with him any longer. Ten want to kill him, but the eldest convinces them to throw Joseph in a pit instead.

One of the Bible's greatest and most epic stories opens with this dream and the subsequent slavery into which Joseph is sold. And speaking of boldness, it is a stunning literary move to devote almost the entire final quarter of Genesis to this one tale. The story of Joseph is packed with the most beloved themes in all of literature: exile, hiding, the hero's journey, rags-to-riches, momentous unveilings, and reunions of brothers long-lost.* As the final story in Genesis, it will develop themes touched upon in every other story, the high points of which we will touch on here.

◇◇◇◇◇◇◇

Jacob loves Joseph more than his other sons; the text says this is because Joseph is "the son of his old age," and it's a safe bet we can add another

---

* For the ideas of veiling and unveiling, Joseph's concealed identity, the way Joseph's clothes throughout the story represent his concealed identity, and Joseph's preoccupation with Benjamin in the second part of this story, I'm drawing upon observations from William Wilson, "Joseph and His Brothers", Lecture at The University of Virginia, Fall 2010.

reason—that Joseph is one of only two of his children by Rachel, Jacob's first love and favorite wife. Jacob's favoritism, as well as Leah's and Rachel's rivalry, causes havoc in the next generation. Competition haunts this story; the older brothers have a higher status in the family than Joseph, and his father's foolish preference for someone beneath them causes them suffering, judging by how much they hate him. Self-justification is in stark relief here; Joseph as their father's favorite is not just an affront to his brothers' status, but to custom and the whole hierarchy of status in world—a hierarchy which God, like Jacob, often subverts. It is wounded pride and scorned entitlement which makes them hate Joseph enough to kill him.

Providence is deeply intertwined with human sinfulness here, perhaps more so than anywhere else in Genesis. If we asked the question of whether God or Joseph's ego gave him the dream, the answer has to be both—if he wasn't at least somewhat arrogant and condescending, his brothers probably would not have wanted to kill him. If we ask whether providence or violence drove Joseph to the pit, the answer would have to be both, too.

The interventionist side of God, which we see in Sodom and Gomorrah and which re-emerges in the Exodus, is not as present here. Instead, God is at work in and through human action, even in human action at its fratricidal worst. Human error—from Jacob's favoritism to Joseph's boasting to the brothers' crime—drives the story forward toward its providential conclusion

Remembering the symbol of clothes as simultaneously covering up and denying one's humanness, the robe Jacob gives Joseph symbolizes both Joseph's pride and the whimsical folly of Jacob. But there is something fitting about it, too; later in the Bible, God will often choose the youngest and weakest for honor or leadership, and Jacob too perceives the value of the least in the strange, new economy of grace.

So his father makes him a fancy robe to remind everyone of his special status, Joseph wears it with barely a shred of bashfulness or self-awareness, and the brothers hate him for it. The dreams don't help. In the first, they are harvesting wheat (or some other grain), and his brothers' bundles of wheat bow down to his. Annoying, but relatively harmless. In the second, as Joseph reports, "'the sun, the moon, and eleven stars were bowing down to me'" (37:9). This galactic homage to Joseph, in which the sun and moon respectively symbolize his father and mother, is too much even for Jacob, who points out its absurdity to his seventeen-year old son.

Joseph has also "told on" his brothers before, bringing a bad report back to Jacob. Telling on someone for doing a poor job is obnoxious in the best of circumstances; coming from a favored younger brother, it would have been especially so. We've seen fatherly acceptance as a symbol for divine acceptance earlier (Jacob and Esau), and here it's no different. Joseph's making accusations of them to their father goes a step beyond basking in his father's favoritism—he is actively subverting his brothers, revealing their faults, and putting them down to maintain and solidify his own high status with Jacob. Thus Joseph is guilty of elevating himself at the expense of the people around him, and both Joseph's accusation and the brothers' coming betrayal of him spring from the same need to be better than others.

◇◇◇◇◇◇◇◇

While all the brothers are out working in the field one day (*sans* Joseph), Jacob sends his favorite out to the field to see how things are going and report back. When the brothers see him coming out to check up on them and give yet another "report" to their father, they become incensed. Well before Joseph comes within earshot, someone proposes they kill him while they are all together and in an isolated place. The eldest, Reuben, disapproves. He doesn't seem to think he can convince them not to kill him, but if he can persuade them to abandon him in a (conveniently nearby) pit instead, perhaps Reuben can double back and rescue him later.

While Reuben's away, possibly wanting no part in his siblings' plot, the brothers spy a caravan approaching and make a last-second change to their plan. They decide to sell Joseph into slavery, not wanting his blood on their hands. There is a certain justice here, even if for the wrong reasons. Joseph, who clearly believed he was better than his brothers and predicted they would one day bow down to him, will become a slave, utterly at the mercy of others. He will become the lowest, and perhaps learn some humility in the process. This rough, human justice—"Let's teach him a lesson"—can easily backfire in everyday life, and often does. But occasionally, it works. God will bring good out of this, too.

By demoting Joseph to a slave, the brothers widen the field of possibilities for God's deliverance. No longer will merely the (second) youngest by birth order be the hero, but moreover, that person will be a slave, the one rejected by his own brothers. Again, the symbol of the coat comes into play: Joseph is stripped of his vanity and pretension and forced to be a mortal, a frail human no different from anyone else. But we cannot idealize slavery as a good human state: God did give Adam and Eve clothes, con-descending to their covering up, to protect them. Nakedness may symbolize vulnerability before God, which is largely good, but it can also imply vulnerability before humans, who will often (in the violent, competitive, self-justifying world after Eden) exploit that nakedness.

Modesty, the resistance to being known physically, can also be understood as a resistance to being known as mere flesh.* Lust might then be seen as the desire to use another's body for self-perpetuating procreation, divorced from its concern for the other person's whole self. And so modesty protects someone from being regarded as mere flesh. Clothes in the case of Adam's and Eve's fig leaves symbolize the desire to hide one's mortal, fleshly humanness, but in the case of God's gift of clothes, they represent protection from being regarded as *mere* flesh, as less than a full human.

Most likely, the author of Genesis would have had no ability to formulate an ethical critique of slavery, but Scripture may speak across time and in excess of direct authorial intent. On this reading of nakedness before humans as vulnerability to exploitation, we see a symbolic unity emerge between selling Joseph into slavery and tearing off his coat. Joseph's vanity is gone, and his pretensions of being more than a human have been stripped, but in his new state, people will treat him as less than a human. Beind reduced to just flesh, being used by others for selfish reasons and without regard to his will: Joseph will suffer near-total degradation here.

An analogy with sexual exploitation (mere flesh) suggests itself here, and we'll see that develop as one of Joseph's masters tries to use him sexually. For now, it will suffice to say that slavery is not an ideal state of learning humility, but rather it entails being reduced to less than a

---

* This builds on Søren Kierkegaard's analysis of modesty in his *The Concept of Anxiety*, trans Albert B. Anderson and Reidar Thomte (Princeton, NJ: Princeton UP, 1980).

human.* He is a commodity to be bought, sold, and put to work where needed.

◇◇◇◇◇◇◇◇

Joseph could not remain in his lofty position lording over his brothers, but neither can he remain sub-human; an equilibrium must emerge. He will rise and fall, find fortune and power in a foreign land, but like his father before him, his estrangement from his family will follow him even into power, and nothing can be resolved until they are reconciled. Whereas the details of Esau's forgiveness of Jacob were sparse, here we will have a fully-fledged drama of remorse and resentment, a complex and down-to-earth examination of how forgiveness and reconciliation occur.

Before that, though, we return to his brothers, who rip his coat and dip it in fresh blood, bringing it back to their father as evidence of Joseph's death. Reuben, the brother who plotted to rescue him, returns and finds the pit empty, and assumes Joseph is dead. Jacob tears his clothes and wears sackcloth, mourning inconsolably over the loss of a favorite child. The brothers have rid themselves, they believe, of their arrogant little brother for good, while Jacob vows to mourn until the day he dies.

Though they cannot see or know it, God is at work. Joseph is now a nomad and an exile, following—albeit unwillingly—the pattern of his father and great-grandfather. He will be gifted with his father's cunning and, as we'll see in the next story, his mother's good looks. And God specializes in favoring slaves and nomads, as Israel's Exodus, which re-capitulates Joseph's journey to Egypt, will later demonstrate. For now, however, we pause, as another brilliant example of frame narration in Genesis interrupts Joseph's story, and Joseph's brother, Judah, goes to see a prostitute.

---

* Commentary on the Christian tradition has largely neglected the potent symbolism, resonating deeply with Eden and with this story, of Jesus being stripped on his way to the cross (and the subsequent casting lots for his clothes) in the Gospel accounts.

Tamar and Potiphar's Wife

(Genesis 38:1–39:20)

We have not seen much in the way of instruction in Genesis thus far. Part of the reason has to do with the fact that the Law, which will be the Bible's first developed statement about ethics, comes later, in the next four books. But another reason, perhaps, is that ethics develop from life, and there are no ethics—no knowledge of good and evil—before the Fall. An ethic is not an arbitrary code, but rather something that embodies a vision of the way the world is supposed to be.

If we could boil down the "ethics" of Genesis to one statement, it would look something like, "of the tree of the knowledge of good and evil you shall not eat" (2:17). Out of the desire to be God comes spiritual self-justification, and this ramifies into all sorts of other human dysfunction. The Law, the locus of Jewish ethics, presents a beautiful model of life lived in a truly human way, in humble reliance upon God. It articulates a vision of a life without a Fall, a picture of a perfect world. As we compare ourselves or others to it, our shortcomings are thrown into sharp relief.

Along these lines, one obligation in ancient Judaism was the expectation that if a woman's husband died, his brother would have children with her to continue the deceased, original husband's line. This story opens with Judah, one of Joseph's brothers, getting married and having three children. Years later, his firstborn (named "Er") is old enough for a wife, so Judah arranges his son's marriage to Tamar. Unfortunately for Tamar, Er dies; Judah tells his second son to marry Er's widow, and shortly after tying the knot, the second son dies, too.

Tamar understandably seems cursed, so much so that Judah suspects his remaining son will also die if he marries her. Judah buys time, telling her to wait until his youngest is a little older. Even after he grows up, Judah balks at arranging the marriage. He has one son left, and this woman was the common denominator among his older children, who died.

Foul play—as in murder—was probably not something to fear at the time. But Tamar being cursed was; it was a more superstitious time. One of the most likely scenarios is that Judah considered Tamar somehow cursed by God. If I were a father, I would rather assume *that* than assume that both my kids were struck down for "wickedness," as the passage states. So there's a dramatic irony building up: we know Tamar is not cursed, but her father-in-law doesn't. He clearly dislikes her, and he later suggests burning her alive when he hears that she is pregnant with a stranger's child. Again, we see human power dynamics at play: the most vulnerable will be given the blame and must take the fall. So after her two husbands' deaths, Tamar is isolated and alone, with Judah's promise for a third husband looking less and less likely as his youngest grows older and remains unmarried.

◇◇◇◇◇◇◇◇

Judah's ethical obligation to marry his youngest son to Tamar reveals the gap between what should happen and what actually does, and it tells us something about Judah's character in the process. He is distancing himself and his family from Tamar, because he does not want to identify with the death which seems to follow her. To come to terms with reality, Judah must identify himself as part of the problem, and Tamar will force this identification to happen.

Sex is the currency of the family, and this story requires us to turn yet again to the development of this theme in Genesis. We saw sexual dysfunction as the fixation on propagating one's own family/self, which undergirds lust. After Judah's eldest, Er, was killed by God for an unspecified reason, Onan, Judah's middle son, marries Tamar. He refuses to have a child with her, however, because the child will not be his. His line will not continue through procreation, but his brother's. So, because Onan is determined that he "would not give offspring to his brother" (38:9), he refuses to impregnate his new wife. Concerned with self-propagation instead of continuing his older brother's legacy (and thus his family's), his actions are dysfunctional, and the story tells us that God killed him, too.

Alone and neglected by her father-in-law, Tamar devises a plan. She will dress up as a prostitute, station herself on the side of a road on which Judah will be traveling, and trick *him* into giving her a child. It works; Judah sees her and goes in to her tent. Afterward, when Judah inquires about compensation, Tamar allows him to send her a baby goat later, on the condition he leaves her his signet, cord and staff.

When Judah does return, she is nowhere to be found, and he decides that recovering his belongings isn't worth the embarrassment of searching further—"Has anyone seen a prostitute around here? She has some of my stuff." So he drops the matter and gets on with his life. About three months later, when he learns that his still unmarried daughter-in-law is pregnant, he is furious. As punishment for this embarrassment, he sentences her to death via the aforementioned burning. As Judah's men detain her, however, Tamar produces evidence that identifies the father of her child-to-be. The belongings are Judah's, and he accepts his fault.

◇◇◇◇◇◇◇◇

Judah's guilt parallels that of his son, Onan. Judah made someone he thought was a prostitute pregnant, leaving no father in the picture. He used her as a mere body, recapitulating themes from Abraham's treatment of Hagar and Joseph's loss of his coat. And when his daughter-in-law is inexplicably pregnant, he decides that she is guilty, deserving of death. But Tamar's ploy works brilliantly: Judah focuses all of his righteous condemnation upon her, which she then forces on him in return.

Humans, from the Garden of Eden on, resist acknowledging guilt. In practice, direct condemnation hardly ever produces true introspection. But stories have a power to cut through that resistance, especially stories which appeal to our sense of justice. So the story Judah hears is that his daughter-in-law, who brought bad luck to his children, has harmed his respectable family yet again. This story focuses his anger, appealing to his self-righteousness, and then the rug is pulled out from under him.

There is no "us versus them," no respectable or unrespectable, no "my family and *that* woman," and no heroes versus villains. Judah, despite his status, is guilty. He even admits that his daughter-in-law is "more in the right than I" (38:26). It's a strange and touching story of repentance, of a man in power being forced to abandon his illusion of moral high ground. This humility produces reconciliation, and he takes both her and their children in as part of the family.

◇◇◇◇◇◇◇◇

We are not mere bodies but spirits, too. One can be used as a body—"I need a hand with this"—but we help people, sit with them, lay a hand on their back, like their appearance or, sometimes, sleep with them out of choice, and that freedom defines relationships. There is no love in obligation, and so long as someone is a slave, he will often be bereft of love from his master. His skills and strengths may be loved, but what of the person underneath? Or even if someone is not a slave, someone with power may still treat that person as something other than a human being. Jacob treated Tamar as a wife for his sons, then as a threat to his family's well-being ("I don't want my third son to die, too"), then as a body to be bought, and finally as a person, a human being no different from himself.

◇◇◇◇◇◇◇◇

With that in mind, we return to Joseph, our cocky and recently-enslaved hero who has been sold to the captain of Pharaoh's guard in Egypt, a man named Potiphar. God gives Joseph unusual skill and good fortune, Potiphar keeps promoting him, and soon he has everything in Potiphar's house running so efficiently that Potiphar has nothing to worry about "but the food that he ate" (39:6). Joseph's extraordinary competence with running a household has bought him favor and honor, but he is still a slave. He is loved for more than just his body by his master, Potiphar; he is also loved for his ability and skill set.

And yet this is still not real love—I think of the movie *Wall Street*, which explores the relationship between a young, budding day trader (played by Charlie Sheen) and his brilliant, expert-investor mentor, Gordon Gekko. The two seem to love each other; Gekko loves the young man's energy and ambition, and Sheen's character loves his mentor's expertise. When things get bad, however, the two men disown each other.

Real love is formed on the basis of vulnerability and honesty, not competence or mere technical skill. Love does not occur through shared strength (strength can fail, or turn out to be a facade), but rather through shared weakness. So Joseph essentially has the love due a brilliant accountant who saves you money on taxes or the chef at your favorite restaurant. But he lacks love for the person underneath, and no matter how highly he rises in Egypt, he will yearn for reconciliation with his family, because they know him for who he really is.

This love of Joseph based primarily upon mere competence finds a strange parallel in his master's wife's several attempts to force him to sleep with her. He is good-looking which, remembering the story of Leah and Rachel, often results in a surface lovability. But even his good looks serve to disguise him; Potiphar's wife cannot see past his attractiveness—she has little genuine care for him.

And so eventually, while her husband is doing the ancient equivalent of running errands or taking a business trip, she seizes Joseph by his clothes and literally will not let him go. Joseph tears himself away, and as in the last story, he loses his clothes. Like the honor and dignity his father accorded him—even though they were misplaced—Joseph's honor as the most valued servant is stripped from him. The symbolism works: Potipher's wife seized onto his clothes (vanity, exterior identity, competence), and Joseph could not express his true self—his freedom—without leaving those things behind. Metaphorically naked, and possibly literally naked, too, he is reduced (or "led back") to being just a body, a servant to be disposed with.

Potiphar's wife is left standing inside with one of her male servants' shirts or pants or robes in her hand—an awkward position. So she improvises and lies, telling her husband that Joseph tried to sleep with her and ran away when she screamed. Again, Joseph is not only stripped of his honor, he is slandered as well; his status is less than human, less than himself. Potiphar's wife has tried to exploit Joseph and then shifted the blame onto him in a way we now see as typical for fallen humanity, especially for those with power. She forces Joseph to take the fall simply because she can, and her husband promptly believes her (who would *want* to imagine it was the other way around?) and has Joseph thrown into prison.

◇◇◇◇◇◇◇

The story of Tamar forms a break in the Joseph narrative, and it is no mistake that afterward, we come back into Joseph's tale at another episode involving attraction and deception. The Tamar story helps make sense of what is going on with Joseph, illuminating his character.

One way to compare these two stories would be to identify Joseph with his brother Judah. They are siblings, after all, and likely pretty similar; also, both are "come on" to. But this parallel reveals a deeper contrast: Judah accepts the offer, and then tries to burn the "prostitute" for getting pregnant. Joseph, on the other hand, refuses to use and be used. He knows that all he has with regard to power and honor depends upon his master's favor, and by comparison, it depends upon the favor of God, who "was with" him and "caused all that he did to prosper" (39:3). Joseph's refusal to give in to lust on moral grounds is not simply abiding by the law or "doing the right thing." On the one hand, it is practical and self-interested; he cannot risk it. Yet on the other hand, his refusal symbolically represents his refusal to self-propagate, to self-justify.

The first, practical motive and the second, symbolic point are in tension. Does Joseph abstain out of respect for himself and for Potiphar's wife (and resistance to symbolic self-perpetuation), or does he abstain out of practical concerns, i.e., a desire to keep hold of his power and position? Probably, to some extent, the story supports both readings. But whatever tension does exist between those two factors is removed when he is thrown into prison; there is no more power or status to maintain.

When Joseph does rise to power, as we will see in the next chapter, it will be through something more gratuitous, more directly God-given, than mere competence. It is only the lowest, with nothing to lose and little to gain, who can abstain from the relentless Adamic preoccupation with status-maintenance and ladder-climbing. And no matter how far he climbs, the problem of his unresolved rift with his brothers will follow him.

On a second look, then, Joseph shares more in common with Tamar than with his brother Judah. Both are scorned and shunned and cast out, and both must fend for themselves. People with more power and status will try to exploit them, Tamar through passive neglect and Joseph through active slandering. Tamar has little to lose, so she tricks her father-in-law into sleeping with her, and as it turns out, she is (mostly) justified in doing so. When the truth of Judah's sin is revealed—both the sin of leaving an apparent prostitute as a single mother *and* (perhaps more significantly) the sin of judging his pregnant daughter-in-law—he acknowledges that she is more right than he, and reconciliation follows.

By comparing Tamar with Joseph, we get a sense for how the redemptive action of Joseph's story must take place. Hiddenness and unveiling, meeting his brothers incognito to prepare them for the truth; acknowledgment of sin by the exploiters, justice for the victims, the urgent need for reconciliation: these will be the patterns which drive the final story in Genesis toward its conclusion. Joseph, like Tamar, has been scorned and isolated. But once more, it is the isolated whom God will exalt, and providence will drive all toward reconciliation.

The Joseph Story, Part Two

(Genesis 39:21–50:26)

Genesis has aged remarkably well, and that's rare. Very few parts of the book seem outdated—it could easily have concerned itself with the professions of farming and shepherding, politics and government, or ancient Near Eastern culture. Many old stories, like Spenser's *Faerie Queene* or Virgil's *Aeneid* or even Dante's *Divine Comedy* cannot be fully appreciated by modern audiences without footnotes or criticism explaining the ways in which the works have "dated" and bridging the historical distance between the story and its readers. Genesis needs less of this bridging than many other works; it concerns fallen human nature and the ways that fallenness manifests itself: competition, blame-shifting, violence, exploitation, and favoritism, among other things. These instincts of the fallen ego are not outdated; they are basic, and they endure.

One theme which has been present in the last few stories, though only latently, is perception, or the problem of how we view other people and God. As a favorite Jewish rabbi famously said, there is a "log in your own eye" which prevents us from seeing others accurately (Mt 7:3). Our perception problem is internal: we see them through the lens of our own self-justification, and thus we judge them too harshly or feel superior to them without good reason.

We all have siblings or coworkers with whom we feel in competition, and we must develop reasons to feel superior to them. Or we have ex-boyfriends or ex-wives whom we must dismiss—"It was never worth it, anyway: she has some serious issues to work through." Or we have bosses who criticize us unfairly and show favoritism to other employees (though secretly, they probably feel that way about us, too). We think our children's teachers don't like them or neglect their learning style. There are logs in our eyes, and the way we see other people and the world is deeply, fundamentally skewed by our desire to appear in the right.

Abraham saw Hagar as a means to an end, and thus allowed Sarah to dismiss her; Cain saw his brother Abel as a judgment upon him, a judgment which could be "removed;" Isaac over-identified with Esau, and Rebekah *way* over-identified with Jacob, who over-identified with Rachel and, therefore, his two sons by her, Joseph and Benjamin. Joseph saw himself through the lens of his Adamic ego, causing him to latch onto his father's special love of him and start believing he was better than his brothers. Instead of seeing an insecure younger brother trying to prove himself, Joseph's brothers saw an arrogant, delusional kid whom the world would be better off without. All are blind to their own faults and hyper-critical of others'.

Thus recognition must be the endpoint of this story, in the way that Judah recognized Tamar and, in recognizing her, recognized himself—as a sinner. His log was removed; he could see clearly. Remembering Eden, any genuine turning toward God on the part of humans will consist in recognizing mortality, recognizing dependence and sinfulness and need of mercy.

As we have observed, God manifests himself to humans first as judge and rescuer. Our deservedness of judgment and our need of rescue—which are really one and the same—are our approaches or entries into relating to God. We must see ourselves properly (taking the logs out of our eyes) in order to see God. Perception, hiddenness, and manifestation form the central themes of this story.

◇◇◇◇◇◇◇◇

We revisit Joseph, who is now in prison after being accused of trying to sleep with Potiphar's wife. His status as head of Potiphar's household has been revoked, and he has been forgotten. His "Midas touch" as a leader and administrator, however, continues to stay with him. Like Potiphar, the person who runs the palace prison soon has few worries or responsibilities; Joseph keeps the establishment running well.

It is surprising that after all his bad fortune, Joseph still seems so level-headed and resourceful. One can imagine that after being thrown into a pit and sold into slavery by his brothers, he probably felt that things were as bad as they could get. Sometimes, however, being stripped of one's identity and pretenses can create contentment with the way things are. That is, sometimes a person finds a strange freedom, even spontaneity, on the other side of intense suffering. The exhausting game of playing God has been lost, and genuine humility—of the sort Abraham had when he chose to sacrifice his son or the humility of Jacob after God dislocated his hip—might ensue.

Thus the theme of being a nomad, robbed of place and time and home to further depend upon God, is here deepened. Joseph will be a nomad geographically, but the harsh fortunes of life will also exile him from his pretensions. Once that fancy robe, such a pain to keep clean and so irritating to others, comes off, his truer self is laid bare. Suffering can strip away our Adamic pride, and what follows is freedom. Thus geographic nomadism will become a symbol—and an enactment of—alienation from one's pride. Suffering has now emerged as a vehicle which God may use to work in the world for good.

◇◇◇◇◇◇◇◇

Soon after Joseph is thrown into prison, Pharaoh has a bad day. He decides that both his baker and his cupbearer—the personal servant who refills the wine and sometimes tests it for poison—should be thrown into prison. Lying in their cells, they have strange dreams which seem prophetic; they ask around for someone who can interpret them. "Do not all interpretations belong to God?," Joseph asks them. "Please tell them to me" (40:8). So the two lay out their dreams: first, the cupbearer sees three vines quickly blossoming—like those time-lapse videos of an African sunrise in *National Geographic* movies—and then ripening. He presses the grapes into a cup and gives it to Pharaoh. Joseph hears him out and declares that Pharaoh will release him in three days.

The poor baker sees that Joseph has given the cupbearer a favorable prognosis, so he decides to go to Joseph, too. There's a fallacy here: Joseph's interpretation has no influence whatsoever over Pharaoh's decision, but the baker just wants to hear some good news. He dreamed he was walking with three baskets stacked on his head, and birds were eating food out of the top one. Joseph's response is unsympathetic in the extreme. Pharaoh will "lift up your head," Joseph tells him, a phrase that means Pharaoh will exalt him and pull him out of his sadness (c. Ps 3:3), and then Joseph callously adds, "from you"—as in beheading (40:19).

I can't help but think of a certain doctor in the TV show *Arrested Development* who constantly gives misleading diagnoses: "I'm sorry to say this, but it's too late for me to do anything for your son... Because Dr. Stein here has already been assigned to his case. You're lucky. He's the best."* What we have with the baker is the opposite—it sounds like great news at first, but turns out to be bad. Joseph certainly has learned some humility, but as we see here, he might still be a bit smug.

Joseph asks the cupbearer to remember him, and the cupbearer forgets. We can imagine Joseph's hope—"Surely he'll remember me! He promised he would; he's probably lobbying Pharaoh for my release right now." And that hope will gradually fade, as he spends the next two years in prison, with no promising way out. Prison, by the way, is horrible. Two full years in prison for a crime someone did not commit would change that person, have a permanent and lasting effect.

It is sometimes easy to lose sight of the vast amounts of time Genesis covers. Skimming the story, we sometimes imagine Joseph had to be patient for a short period, but could endure knowing that God would save him. This is not the way real life works, however much we may want it to. Sometimes, the wait is crushing, with no end in sight. We know God often brings good out of suffering—but try telling that to someone who has just gone through a divorce or lost a family member. The story here is not as tidy as we might like, and any picture of Joseph as someone happily waiting in prison, knowing God will deliver him, is misguided. God's work in suffering does not minimize the suffering or make it any easier to bear. For suffering to work for good, it must first really *be* suffering, and the reality of being in prison, falsely accused and forgotten by Pharaoh, would probably not have been particularly palatable to the prisoner.

◇◇◇◇◇◇◇

After two years, Pharaoh himself starts having disturbing dreams about starving cows and crops that eat each other. Seven fat cows appear and

---

* "Sword of Destiny", Season 2, Episode 14, from *Arrested Development*

are eaten by seven skinny cows, but the skinny cows don't get any bigger. Then seven good ears of grain grow on a stalk, and seven withered ones grow up afterward and eat them. This troubles Pharaoh, and he complains frequently, but no one can give him a satisfactory explanation. His cupbearer ventures a suggestion; to paraphrase, "remember that time you threw me into prison? There was a guy—I think he's still there—who predicted accurately that I would be let out, and you would have the baker killed. Probably should've mentioned that sooner."

So Pharaoh demands that Joseph come and try to tell him what his dreams mean. After the prisoner shaves (remember Tom Hanks's matted hair in *Castaway*?) and changes clothes (people probably didn't get to bathe much in ancient jail), he comes to Pharaoh and stands at attention: "I have heard it said of you that when you hear a dream you can interpret it," Pharaoh says (41:15). Joseph claims that the skill isn't actually his, but belongs to a foreign deity ("God") who works through him. But Pharaoh just wants to move on to the skinny cows and hungry wheat.

Joseph interprets them: Egypt will have seven years of good harvest and fat livestock, and then it will have seven years of famine which will destroy all of the abundance of the earlier years. Pharaoh needs to appoint someone to manage the impending disaster, someone who can store up surplus during the good years and then ration it out during the bad years. Pharaoh thinks for a while about who would be the best candidate—preferably someone "in whom is the spirit of God" (41:37)—and settles on Joseph, whom he promptly frees from slavery, arranges a good marriage for, and gives total authority in Egypt.

A few points of analysis are necessary here. First, Joseph has learned not to trust himself; his skills come from God, and being a nomad and a slave has given him perspective. He knows his dependence upon God. Second, Pharaoh recognizes God's favor is with Joseph: the newly freed prisoner is more "discerning and wise" than anyone else, mainly because "God has shown [him] all this" (41:39). Joseph has already matured to the point of being a biblical hero, a patriarch, through humility and dependence upon God. In terms of his skills and fortunes, the log is solidly out of his eye—he can see, accurately, that all he has is a gift, and that he cannot claim any of his talents for himself. This attitude will make him the hero throughout the story. Third, this clear, humble perspective is what allows him to rightly interpret dreams.

We have here a "meta" moment, stories (the dreams) within a story, and Joseph is the master interpreter. He can "read" the meaning of the dreams precisely because he knows that all comes from God; he will not see what he wants to see, nor what Pharaoh wants him to see.* His freedom from his own pride allows him to read the world accurately.

◇◇◇◇◇◇◇◇

In closing out this "dream sequence," however, we still have a problem. When Joseph has children, he names his firstborn Manasseh, which means, "to forget," because "'God has made me forget my hardship and all my father's house'" (41:51).† Forgetting is not the same as reconciliation, which this story drives toward. Joseph's last remaining blind spot is his family; the name may mean "to forget," but ironically, the name is in Hebrew—he is still speaking his family's language. "Don't think about a white bear," as the self-defeating saying goes. He tries to avoid thinking about it, consoling himself with all that God has given him in Egypt, but the problem will not, in this story, go away.

Why can't the story just progress to God blessing Joseph, and end there? The lowest has been exalted, someone has gone from slave to second-in-command of what was likely the most powerful civilization at the time, and God has been glorified by Pharaoh. It would seem like a good place to conclude. But Joseph is not yet fully known. Just as the pride of his father's favoritism—symbolized by the robe—disguised his true self, so too Joseph's competence disguises him here. He is known as an extraordinarily capable person, someone who is wise, and someone in whom the spirit of God dwells.

Instead of his father's robe or his slave garments, he is now "arrayed in garments of fine linen" and wears "a gold chain around his neck" (41:42). He is honored throughout Egypt for his competence, but Joseph has yet to be known and loved in his weakness. He was not known in weakness as a child either. He always felt he should "put his best foot forward" and persuade his brothers to love him for his honored position in the family. Later, he is exploited for his weakness—known as weak

---

* Many dream interpreters and prophets of ancient times tended to keep their jobs by telling their master what he wanted to hear. Self-preservation colored their interpretations, and one can imagine they grew so adept at this rosy point of view that many of them may have forgotten they were just flattering him in the first place.

† Again, meanings of names are taken from the notes to *The New Oxford Annotated Bible*.

but not loved—symbolized by Potiphar's wife's attempt to use him. And here in Egypt, while he is loved, it is merely love for his competence and leadership; the Egyptians seem to value him mainly for his strengths.

So Joseph's narrative arc is incomplete and unfinished; he must be valued in his whole self, which will necessarily encompass his weakness. And the only people capable of valuing him in that way are those who know his flaws best: his lost brothers back from Israel, the family he has tried so hard to forget. He will wear his strengths and status; the motif of clothing as a disguise of *true* identity gives us an entry into the story's meaning, as well as into its unresolved tensions.

◇◇◇◇◇◇◇◇

Egypt is in a state of famine, and as with the flood story, nature's good and ill fortunes symbolize the limits of human power and the overarching sovereignty of the divine. Not only will this famine threaten Egypt, but also it will bring Joseph's siblings—now a distant but harrowing memory—back into his life. Even Pharaoh, as powerful as he is, cannot prevent a famine; Joseph, no matter how much he would like to forget, cannot escape the unresolved conflict between himself and his distant brothers

The famine drives his family to Egypt, where God's interpretation of Pharaoh's dream, through Joseph, will save Jacob and his other sons. Egypt, however, is a couple hundred miles away, depending on their route. Travel at the time was not easy; robbers or slavers, natural disasters or diseases were likely a few of many dangers on a long trip with remote stretches of desert and wilderness. Jacob, still grieving the death of Joseph, sends ten of his children along, but he will not part with his youngest, Benjamin, who in his mind is Rachel's last remaining son.

Joseph meets his brothers and chooses to remain anonymous. Since he is now a powerful figure and the balance of power has shifted, he treats them harshly; after all, he likely feels some vengeful hostility toward them. He accuses them of being spies who have "'come to see the nakedness of the land,'" an accusation which fits well with their earlier stripping of Joseph's robe (42:12). After throwing them in prison for three days—"Who's a prisoner *now*"—he tells them he will test the veracity of their protests by forcing them to bring him their youngest brother, Benjamin.

It is impossible at this stage to assess Joseph's motives. The most likely explanation would be a desire to see Benjamin, who is his closest living sibling (the others are from different mothers) and also someone who, as the youngest, may have been less involved in the decision to sell Joseph into slavery. As much as he has tried to forget, there is certainly a part of Joseph that wants to see and reconcile with his family. If it were only spite he felt, he would have either had them killed or sent away, permanently empty-handed.

The movement of repentance is already starting to happen. The brothers realize, to some extent, that Benjamin, as the youngest and therefore one with the lowest status, is the favored son. Feeling responsible for Benjamin's well-being, and fearful that he may be threatened, they think back to another time when they were responsible to a younger brother and failed. We learn, heart-wrenchingly, that Joseph had "pleaded" with them in "anguish" (42:2). "Let me out—please. Please!" we can imagine him crying, helpless with absolute, physical, primal fear. Now that Joseph has the power, he vindictively forces them to plead with him. Their fear makes them remember what they had done to Joseph, and the brothers' realization of wrongdoing moves Joseph so much that the stern judge, who holds their lives in his hands, must excuse himself and find solitude before the tears start pouring down his face.

◇◇◇◇◇◇◇◇

Now composed, and having hardened himself against weak sentiment, Joseph gets back to business. He forces his brothers to leave him with a hostage, ordering Simeon to be left behind and tied up. He then gives them their grain, to take back to feed their ageing father and younger brother. And, through some inexplicable impulse, he has their money secretly put back in their bags. It may or may not have been an act of sentimental generosity, but its immediate effect is to inspire terror. It appears they have unintentionally stolen grain from Egypt or, at the least, been purposely framed for doing so—and Simeon's life is on the line. Still, Jacob will not let Benjamin go, so the brothers cannot return. As they eat grain, Simeon languishes in an Egyptian prison, and Joseph wonders where they have gone.

The story continues to reveal new details about the past. We did not know that Joseph had "pled" with them until his brothers recollect the event in Egypt, five chapters later. As the brothers come to their senses and re-member themselves as sinners, the victim, Joseph, becomes clearer to them, more human. The narrative employs the same device here, in the brothers' conversation with their father. We did not know Joseph asked about his father's health; the narrative withheld that detail until now. And again, as the brothers are growing more concerned with their father's bereavement and their youngest brother's value, the family dynamics deepen; more about their relationships comes to light.

In a parallel move, we as readers learn more; as the story's drama heightens, the emotional stakes are raised, and Joseph's suppressed emotions toward his family come more and more into the fore. Repentance involves remembering the past, perceiving accurately how things happened and, by extension, who we are, even when these memories reveal things we do not want to remember. In this sophisticated literary device of retroactive narration, as the crisis of the present deepens, the past becomes more alive, more pressing, and more real.

As the brothers' repentance deepens, the power dynamics become reversed. Reuben, the eldest, swears that he will forfeit both of his children if harm comes to Benjamin. Judah, who has already been humbled and come to know his weakness in the Tamar story, also offers to bear the blame if harm comes to Benjamin. They will honor their father by protecting his youngest, who is another "child of Jacob's old age" and another favorite. No longer will they blame their honored brother for Jacob's favoritism, because self-justifying competition is losing its foothold within and among them. Instead, there is identification: "Benjamin's safety will be my safety; Benjamin's harm will be my harm." And again, Reuben offers his children's lives for Benjamin rather than his own. The implication is clear: no longer will Benjamin be just a brother to him, but Judah will also treat him as a son.* Jacob still refuses to send his youngest, but when the food runs out, they have no choice but to take Benjamin with them to Egypt; otherwise they will all die.

◇◇◇◇◇◇◇◇

Upon their return, the brothers are invited into Joseph's house, and their sense of guilt over Joseph, which informs their fear for Benjamin, skews

---

* This identification, which finds its highest expression in self-sacrifice, is another theme from the Hebrew Scriptures which could perhaps be consulted more in New Testament interpretation.

their perception: the great Egyptian leader will seize them and, tellingly, make slaves of them, they fear. The Egyptian leader is not yet home; the men rush to apologize and explain themselves to his steward. In response to their fear, they receive grace—the man tells them that their family's deity ("God") must have given them their money. Where they suspected accusation, they are met with a gift from God.

Everything is made ready for the great man's arrival, and Joseph, still curious and concerned for his family, asks about their father. Incidentally, they bow down to him—the narrative's nod to Joseph's dream from years ago—and watch in fascination as Egypt's second-in-command praises their youngest brother and then hurriedly leaves the room. Once again, Joseph sobs in private. Once again, he sternly composes himself, conceals his emotions, and poses as the competent Egyptian leader. The brothers seat themselves according to birth hierarchy, with Reuben in the most honored position. Formally, the family hierarchy is honored. And that hierarchy serves as a backdrop for what happens next, when the youngest, Benjamin, receives five times as much food as the rest. Everyone drinks wine, and they enjoy the company of this strangely gracious Egyptian who had brutally accused them before.

Joseph's identity, however, is still veiled; reconciliation has yet to occur. But Joseph's resentment of them has not abated. Knowing how much they value Benjamin, and how much his father does, he will torture them by once again making them guilty of losing the favorite child. He places his expensive silver in Benjamin's bag, and he orders his men to follow the brothers as they leave, accusing them of stealing the silver. They swear that no one has taken it, and to prove their sincerity, they make a deal with Joseph that anyone with the cup in his bag will die. Benjamin, their father's favorite child with whom he could not part, is marked with the cup. Joseph, in the guise of the imposing Egyptian, tells them he will take Benjamin as a slave rather than kill him.

◇◇◇◇◇◇◇◇

Joseph's identification with Benjamin is central to the story's meaning.[*] The identification is established on the basis of their shared mother and shared status as the two youngest. Joseph now will see if his brothers

---

[*] Again, Joseph's identification with Benjamin and Benjamin's exalted status as the younger are ideas taken from William Wilson, University of Virginia, ibid.

truly regret what they did to him; he will make them relive their crime in all its horror. Watching their reactions to Benjamin's enslavement will allow him to gauge how they feel about the brother they made a slave long ago. The brothers, in an act of grace, all offer to be slaves, willingly identifying themselves with the youngest. And because Joseph is creating a situation which so neatly mirrors his own enslavement, love shown to Benjamin becomes, vicariously, love shown to Joseph, too. But he will push his brothers still further: he rejects their offer to be his slaves, takes Benjamin, and leaves them.

The brothers' devotion (and remorse) does not allow them to give Benjamin up so easily. They go further than offering to be Joseph's slaves; they do everything in their power to get Benjamin back. Judah, who has learned to see himself in those with lesser status than him (Tamar again), goes to Joseph's house and makes a special plea for Benjamin, appealing to his father's love of the boy and, perhaps, stirring Joseph's memories of his father's love—long ago—for Joseph himself. Judah again begs the great Egyptian leader to allow him to become a slave in Benjamin's place.

It is a beautiful and utterly true moment of repentance—of humility and conviction leading to gracious self-sacrifice. Remembering his father's love and experiencing, vicariously, his brothers' love of him, "Joseph could no longer control himself" (45:1). He finally reveals his true self to his brothers, who have already loved him through Benjamin. His veneer of authority cracks, then shatters; he weeps so loudly that everyone within the whole palace hears it. And when he unveils himself, the brothers are terrified. They deserve judgment, and they are about to get it. Justice has come full circle, and that circle is about to close up neatly with their enslavement or death. Joseph responds to their stunned, terrified silence:

> "'I am your brother, whom you sold into Egypt. And now do not be distressed, or angry with yourselves, because you sold me here; for God sent me before you to preserve life. For the famine has been in the land these two years; and there are five years in which there will be neither plowing nor harvest...' Then he fell upon his brother Benjamin's neck and wept, while Benjamin wept upon his neck. And he kissed all his brothers and wept upon them; and after that his brothers talked with him" (45:4-15).

The passage is among the most moving in all of Genesis. Joseph is known at last in his weakness, his weeping, and he finds real love from his family. His brothers, likewise, are finally known in all their horrible betrayal, but Joseph loves them still, sobs into their shoulders, and forgives them, even urging them not to be angry with themselves, nor ashamed. Their conviction and guilt were prerequisites for them to show love to Benjamin, the fulcrum of reconciliation, but now that reunion has happened, the time for guilt is past. The long exile is behind them, the exile of Joseph from family and his real, human identity, as well as the exile of his brothers from sound conscience and real forgiveness. Joseph invites them all to live in Egypt, and Jacob, who cannot believe his ears, finally rouses himself; his spirit is "revived," and he climbs into the wagon Joseph sent to carry him on the journey. Along the way, he receives a promise from God: "Joseph's own hand shall close your eyes" (46:4).

◇◇◇◇◇◇◇◇

For seventeen years the family lives together, until Jacob at last dies. After all his deceit and fear and running and bereavement, Jacob blesses Joseph's children and then his own, each in turn, and breathes his last with his son by his bedside, closing his eyes. After he dies, Joseph's brothers become afraid, wondering whether Joseph tolerated them merely for the sake of their father, whom he loved. But before Jacob died, we learn, he desired not only his son to be reconciled to him, but also he wanted his other sons' crimes against Joseph forgiven. When the family's leader and patriarch dies, it is left to the next generation to relate to each other apart from him, and Joseph forgives them once more, and they all cry together. His brothers bow down to him and offer themselves as Joseph's slaves, and Joseph again tells them that they are forgiven: "Even though you intended to do harm to me, God intended it for good, in order to preserve a numerous people, as he is doing today" (50:20).

Providence works in all our manifold dysfunction. God allows us to see ourselves as the least (that is, as fully human) and recognize our dependence upon him. In identifying with the lowest, we see ourselves in the worst actions of human nature—in the pride of Adam's first sin, in the ambition of Jacob, as victims through Joseph's slavery or as perpetrators through his brothers—and there we see ourselves, too, as both known and loved and, through that love, reconciled. Joseph's words to his brothers form a perfect closing statement for Genesis: though Adamic, self-justifying and violent humans do each other harm, God works all for good, to preserve a numerous people, as he is still doing today.

Postscript

These stories begin with the Fall, which included *all* of humanity. Likewise, Cain's sin served as a symbol for all of humanity, and in the flood, God destroyed all of humanity—except for Noah. Throughout the redemptive parts of the book—the parts in which God is working to reconcile humanity to himself—he works through a specific family, which will develop into a specific, chosen nation. But whatever happened to *all* of humanity?

At the close of the Joseph story, we see God's special preference for the least, the lowest in status or reputation or even morality. The brothers are only reconciled once they learn to recognize the value of their little brother, Benjamin. If God chose the rich, the poor would be excluded, because we fallen humans would likely imagine that his choice was based on merit. If God chose the powerful, history's victims would be excluded, because we would want to imagine that we earn God's favor by accruing wealth and influence. And if God chose only the righteous, those who cannot help but sin continually would be excluded, because we all want to be valued for our strengths.

But if God chooses the poor, the helpless, and the sinners of the world, his unconditional favor toward all becomes manifest, and it forces itself into our field of vision. We cannot identify with those who seem to be doing better than we are, because we want what they have, and we cannot attain it. So it is only through love of the weak, to whom we can all relate, that God's love for all humans shows itself as clear, firm, and utterly true. And thus it must be through God's love specifically of *sinners* that he represents the whole of humanity.

As noted in the introduction, if we read Genesis merely as great literature, it resists that categorization, demanding to be taken as something *more* than just great literature. This "more" turns out to be, in part, the providence of God, the way in which he works through human sinfulness. But even the remarkable series of events which turns Joseph's enslavement into the preservation "of a numerous people" (50:20) leaves open the question of what happens to Abraham, Isaac, and Jacob after they die.

There is a gap, in other words, between the partial, human reconciliation with family at the moment of death, and the full, complete, perfect and all-encompassing reconciliation which would bring all of Adam's wayward family back to itself, to each other, and to God. This gap could be summarized as our own weakness, our share in Adam's estrangement, and human experience can be neither complete nor finally good until this gap is closed, and hopes fulfilled. Yet just as Adam fell trying to bridge the gap between God and man, so too a final and perfect reconciliation requires us first to recognize that there is a gap, to recognize our humanness, frailty, dysfunction, and mortality.

Though it is an inherent human tendency to rush toward self-improvement or self-advancement or virtue or knowledge of God, these stories first direct our eyes toward the gap between ourselves and God. Our fallenness, our identity with Adam, appears in our self-driven attempts to close this gap, since those attempts differ little from Adam's original grasping upward, at the fruit, and they reveal our desire to know good from evil, to be like God.

Stories allow us to identify ourselves with weakness, to see our own faults and failures. While these blind spots cause us immense pain and trouble, they are, after the Fall, a central part of what it means to be human. Just as God demonstrates his love for all people through his love of the weak, so too he demonstrates his love for the total human person through his love in the full knowledge of our destructive habits and traits. God knows us fully; he knows our most toxic and damaging thoughts, feelings, and actions. And his love acquires its fullness and depth only in view of how far we have strayed. This love is independent of our recognition of it, but we do well to learn of it, to take it to heart and live in its light.

That love only becomes clear to us, however, when we ourselves acknowledge the darkest and worst parts of ourselves. Only then are we given the vision of the full depth of God's love for us. Stories allow us to do this; like the story Tamar tells of a man who goes in to a prostitute, or the story Joseph tells about a youngest brother about to be taken into slavery, the biblical narrative teaches us about the world, but first it teaches us about ourselves. These stories take the proverbial logs out of our eyes by forcing us to recognize them, and such self-knowledge *as sinners* clarifies our view of the world. The blurry, tree-like figures we see, walking around (Mk 8:24) resolve just a little more into human shapes; our vision slightly sharpens, and as it does, we realize more and more just how blurry the world around us really appears.

◇◇◇◇◇◇◇◇

There is a passage in Dante's *Divine Comedy* in which the narrator, who is traveling through hell, a place of judgment for those who sin, describes how God himself entered and carried Adam's soul away, out into eternal fellowship with him. Adam, who tried to exceed his limits and be more than human, and thereby became something less than human; Adam, who died with consuming regret in memory of perfect fellowship with others and with God, but only as a distant dream—this same Adam was restored, and even he was forgiven and reconciled.

How does God bring all of humanity to himself? At this point, it is impossible not to cross over into Christianity. If choosing the least makes clear God's love of the whole of humanity, what does it mean for God to actually *become* the least? If God's love of us can only be taken to heart once we see his love within the worst of our sin, what would it mean for God himself to "be sin" for us (2 Cor 5:21)? It can only mean a full reconciliation, about which we can speak few words besides affirming how "much more" than any human word such a reconciliation would be (Rm 5:17).

Genesis follows a model of death and resurrection, with its characters constantly forced to die to pretensions, judgments of others, and their own illusory moral high ground—in short, to the self, who is Adam and Cain, Sarah and Hagar, Jacob and Esau and Joseph, every single day. After the burden of Adamic pride is stripped from them, as it inevitably will be from us, much good and freedom and spontaneity and love for others can follow.

And yet we resist experiences and stories which threaten our pride; we protect it. But to see ourselves properly, as weak and yet strong, sinners and yet righteous, known and yet loved, just such a threat to vanity must be allowed in. Stories are like surgeons, probing our weaknesses in order to heal them, showing our distance from God and other humans and the person we'd like to be, in order to bridge that distance. As T.S. Eliot wrote in *East Coker*:

> *"The wounded surgeon plies the steel*
> *That questions the distempered part;*
> *Beneath the bleeding hands we feel*
> *The sharp compassion of the healer's art*
> *Resolving the enigma of the fever chart.*
>
> *Our only health is the disease*
> *If we obey the dying nurse*
> *Whose constant care is not to please*
> *But to remind of our, and Adam's curse,*
> *And that, to be restored, our sickness must grow worse."*

Despite the divine surgeon's careful and gentle healing, we never fully recognize our weakness; at least I, for one, do not. The stories which teach us our weakness still look blurry, like trees, walking. This is one reason why stories hold an inexhaustible reservoir of meaning—and why it is such good news that they do. Reading over and over again, coming back to the primal images and emotions of human life, our weakness becomes clearer. We move from humility to greater humility, and since greater weakness magnifies the depth of God's grace, our movement from humility to humility is simultaneously a movement "from one degree of glory to another" (2 Cor 5:18).

Even in the world's best stories—even in those we believe to be divinely inspired—our vision is blurry, and we resist being taught our weakness. And so God's grace must exceed even stories which demonstrate both our faults and the love of a God who is fully aware of them. Our reminders of Adam's curse, which saturate these stories and, at every moment, impose themselves in our lives, are helpful to us, and they draw us toward God, but something more remains to be said.

We do not need merely a demonstration of the love of God, but an enactment of it in our lives, one which happens independently of our paltry ability to recognize it. Jacob died with his favorite person in the world closing his eyes for him, and though Jacob never knew it, that same person wept on his body after he died. We may or may not see God's work during our lives, when we only know in part. We may not see it clearly in our moment of death, when we cannot do or think or say a thing. But in life and in death, God himself weeps over us, and he works for us as he did for Jacob:

> *"'Out of Zion will come the Deliverer;*
> *He will banish ungodliness from Jacob.'*
> *'And this is my covenant with them,*
> *When I take away their sins.'"*

– Romans 11:26-27

About Mockingbird

Founded in 2007, Mockingbird is an organization devoted to connecting the Christian faith with the realities of everyday life in fresh and down-to-earth ways. We do this primarily, but not exclusively, through our publications, conferences and online resources. In addition to Eden and Afterward, our titles include PZ's Panopticon: An Off-the-Wall Guide to World Religion, The Mockingbird Devotional: Good News for Today (and Every Day), Grace in Addiction: The Good News of Alcoholics Anonymous for Everybody, This American Gospel: Public Radio Parables and the Grace of God, The Gospel According to Pixar, and Judgment and Love. We also publish The Mockingbird, a quarterly magazine.

To find out more, visit us at mbird.com or e-mail us at info@mbird.com.

Made in the USA
San Bernardino, CA
23 May 2014